ELIJAH

A MAN LIKE US

DAVID ROPER

Elijah: A Man Like Us
Copyright © 1997 David Roper

Original edition titled *Seeing Through* copyright © 1995 by David Roper

Discovery House Publishers is affiliated with RBC Ministries, Grand Rapids, Michigan 49512

Unless indicated otherwise, Scripture quotations are from the *Holy Bible: New International Version,* copyright © 1973, 1978, 1984, International Bible Society. Used by permission of Zondervan Bible Publishers.

Library of Congress Cataloging-in-Publication Data

Roper, David, 1933—
    [Seeing through]
    Elijah : a man like us / David Roper.
        p. cm.
    Originally published: Seeing through. Sisters, OR : Multnomah Book, © 1995.

    ISBN 1-57293-031-4

    1. Elijah (Biblical prophet) 2. Christian life. I. Title.
[BS580.E4R59 1998]
222'.5092—dc21   97-46005
                                                        CIP

03
CHG
3 5 7 9 10 8 6 4 2

Contents

Foreword

When God's people slide into the ditch of conformity to their sinful surroundings, a man of Elijah's bravado is required.

For many of Christ's followers in shouting distance of the twenty-first century, the ancient prophet has been banished to the basement files. Now, David Roper ushers readers into a powerful revisit with this paladin of the past.

God unleashed Elijah into unprecedented opposition. Israel's king and queen blithely ignored divine laws; their people concurred and cooperated. When it looked like the prophets of Yahweh were down for the count, the messenger from Gilead showed up at the palace. Affirming the word of the Lord with God-breathed intensity, he stood alone by faith. The royal renegades flared with schemes of retaliation. No twentieth-century stage or screen can match the high drama of the confrontation.

Winston Churchill once observed that "a foolish consistency is the hobgoblin of little minds." Elijah the Tishbite had big ideas. No puny manmade gods would defraud *his* nation. Our flabby, mired-in-the-mud timidity desperately needs a generous tug of Elijah's rash rectitude. Because he was a man like us in his passions, we can become like him in our prayers—the ultimate resource for spiritual impact.

7

Only a man who himself burns with malcontent over our own mediocrity can rekindle the prophet's fire. David Roper has warmed these pages with his unique recall of pertinent quotations, his skill at aiming literary arrows to blast our complacency. We flinch at the writer's deadly accuracy.

In our day of superficial and secular thinking, here is a Gillette-edge of refreshing challenge. Ours is a universal conspiracy not to take the Scriptures seriously. If it's old, we trash it. Our mania for "relevance" demands cheap fashion.

My reading of Roper returns me to a long-ago classroom. His writing skills fairly begged to be broadcast. I am honored to have planted some seeds on his fertile soil, to have watched them grow and reproduce. Now, weathered by the rugged American West, he comes into print again with a hot branding iron.

Elijah, Roper-style, is the man for this hour.

Howard G. Hendricks

Introduction

There arose a prophet like fire,
Whose word was like a burning furnace . . .
By the word of God he shut up the heavens;
Fire descended three times,
How awesome you are, Elijah.

—Ben Sirach

There was no one quite like Elijah.

Yes, there were other prophets—even more prominent ones. But Elijah's "spirit and power" were the standard by which all others were measured.

He appeared at a critical moment in Israel's history, just as she was about to slide over a precipice and plunge to her doom. Baal worship and the orgiastic rites that accompanied this devotion had spiritually gutted the nation. The priests and priestesses who presided over the cult had settled into every nook and cranny of national life.

Yahweh's altars had been dismantled.

His prophets were in hiding.

His worshipers were a mere handful, scattered and intimidated by the scope of evil around them, their existence known only to God.

And behind it all was the diabolical duo—Ahab and Jezebel.

9

Elijah ambled out of the backcountry of Gilead and into Ahab's court, armed only with the confidence that God was unquestionably alive. Single-handedly, he checked the terrible progress of Israel's evil, turning them away from their figment gods and back to the living and true God.

The gruesome and violent altars of Baal were torn down and replaced by enduring reminders of God's goodness. Courage was inspired in the timid remnant of the faithful. Schools were opened for the training of a new generation of prophets, and an impetus was given toward godliness that endured for generations to follow.

Elijah was the greatest of the prophets. His name was synonymous with success for nine hundred years after his death, his fame surpassing the greatest and most famous of Israel's leaders.

Malachi could find no better symbol of the fabled forerunner of the Messiah than to compare him with the prophet of Carmel: "I will send you the prophet Elijah before that great and dreadful day of the LORD comes" (Malachi 4:5).

Four hundred years later, Gabriel, standing in the Holy Place, said of John the Baptist, "He will go on before the Lord in the spirit and power of Elijah" (Luke 1:17).

When John's movement was stirring the land and the people were thinking that Malachi's Elijah had come back to earth, a deputation was sent from Jerusalem to ask, "Are you Elijah?" (John 1:21). And then, when one greater than John appeared and set everyone to pondering his sayings, the people concluded, though wrongly, "He is Elijah" (Mark 6:15).

These attributions speak to Elijah's towering greatness. What he did was unique in the annals of faith.

Would that we were like him.

Would that God would put his spirit and power upon us, that we might become the source by which the fullness of God can be poured out to weary and empty men and women in our culture.

If it could be shown that Elijah's place in history was the result of some unusual talent or personal charisma or inherent quality he possessed, then his story has no meaning for us. But if, to use James's expression, "Elijah was . . . *just like us*" (James 5:17, emphasis added), if his accomplishments were based on sources of strength and qualities of life that *anyone* can acquire, then his story is our story as well.

The nation sank deeper and deeper into the shadows
and edged nearer and nearer judgment.
But God is never at a loss.
He provides for every eventuality.
When things look most dark and dangerous,
when evil men and women have done their worst,
then God can begin.
And he usually begins in a very small place
by preparing a very obscure person.

Chapter One

The Worst of Times, The Best of Times

We seem to see our flag unfurled
Our champion waiting in his place
For the last battle of the world,
The Armageddon of the race.
—John Greenleaf Whittier

It was the best of times, or, depending on your outlook, the foulest and most depraved.

Israel's fortunes had seldom looked better, and yet—the man at the helm of state was none other than the childish and fiendish Ahab.

King Ahab was brilliant, daring, charming, and rich—everything but true. His Hebrew name suggests "God is a close relative," but his life belied his name. According to Israel's historian, he did more evil in the sight of the Lord

13

than any other man (see 1 Kings 16:29–34), and he did so as the pawn of his shady lady, the infamous Jezebel.

Ahab married Jezebel as a matter of political convenience. He wanted to consolidate his position vis-à-vis Phoenicia, Israel's rich and illustrious neighbor to the west. Phoenicia enjoyed wealth and luxury on a scale unprecedented in the ancient world. Her colonies dotted the Mediterranean, her navies ruled the seas, circumnavigating Africa and trading in far-off exotic places. Phoenicia's name was a byword for affluence and influence.

Ahab wanted a piece of the action.

He got it.

And undoubtedly more than he'd bargained for.

By taking the young and beautiful Jezebel as his wife, the son of Omri earned a lasting place in Israel's history books. As the biblical writer put it: "He not only considered it trivial to commit the sins of Jeroboam son of Nebat [who joined Israel to idols], but he also married Jezebel daughter of Ethbaal king of the Sidonians, and began to serve Baal and worship him" (1 Kings 16:31).

In taking a foreign wife, Ahab was following the example of his illustrious forefather Solomon, who entered into numerous royal marriages for all the wrong reasons.

King Solomon . . . loved many foreign women besides Pharaoh's daughter—Moabites, Ammonites, Edomites, Sidonians and Hittites. They were from nations about which the LORD had told the Israelites, "You must not intermarry with them, because they will surely turn your hearts after their gods." (1 Kings 11:1–2)

Ahab, however, carried Solomon's folly a quantum leap further. Though Solomon's exotic wives brought their gods with them and the king compromised his faith by capitulating to their demands, his brides (at least) never tried to force their idolatry on the people of Israel.

Jezebel, however, was made of sterner stuff.

This crafty, unscrupulous woman came from a long line of monstrous tyrants. Her father was the cruel and vicious Ethbaal, who murdered his way to the throne of the city-state of Sidon by assassinating his brothers. He was the child of his bitter and pitiless religion and, according to Menander, a Greek writer, its high priest. His name, "Eth-baal" says it all: Taken at face value it means, "(I'm) with Baal."

Jezebel's name is also associated with the worship of Baal and was probably taken from a line in a Phoenician poem:

> *Where is Baal, the Overcomer?*
> *Where is the Prince, the Lord of the earth?*

The question, "Where is the Prince?" In Phoenician is *iy-zebel* and was the name given to Jezebel, the Sidonian princess. She too was a consummate Baal worshiper.

When the Phoenician moving van backed up to the palace in Samaria, Jezebel moved in bags, baggage, and Baals. From that day forward, there would be no doubt as to who wore the royal pants in the family. Ahab was utterly dominated by this unprincipled woman.

One ancient writer characterized Ahab as an example of one who, though he had been a witness by day to Elijah's character and God's faithfulness, "yet by night drank the poison of his wife Jezebel's vicious persuasion." Some men, it seems, will be just as wicked as their women want them to be.

Jezebel was an unusually ardent missionary of the Baal cult. She established a Baal site at Jezreel, Israel's summer capital, supporting its 450 priests out of her own purse. Then she induced her addle-brained husband to build a huge temple in Samaria, large enough to house great crowds of idol worshipers (see 2 Kings 10:21).

Groves, shrines, and temples of Baal and his lovers—Anat, Astarte, and Asherah—began to dot the landscape, while Yahweh's altars were ground into powder. The land was filled with Jezebel's lascivious priests and the temple prostitutes who plied their trade on every street in the nation.

Jezebel's reign was characterized by an overt and pervasive hatred of Israel's God. She poisoned the minds of the people with lies and false teaching generated by her prophets and then, intoxicated by her animosity, moved on to more unmistakable means of suppression: She began systematically "killing off the LORD's prophets" (1 Kings 18:4).

The anointed prophets were hounded without mercy.

The schools of the prophets were boarded up.

Many perished.

Others hid "in caves and holes in the ground" (Hebrews 11:38).

Brave Obadiah was able to save only a few of his brother prophets by secreting them away in the network of limestone caves around Mount Carmel. Out of all Israel, only seven thousand men and women refused to bow the knee to Baal (1 Kings 19:18). But even these were so paralyzed by fear the nation hardly knew of their existence.

Baalism became Israel's state religion.

Baal worship was the most degraded religious system ever devised—and Phoenician Baalism was the worst of the lot. It's thought by some scholars that the Phoenician coast was settled by the refugees from Sodom and Gomorrah who fled the Valley of Sidim when their cities were destroyed and who brought with them their depraved culture.

The Phoenician version of Baal worship was deemed evil even by other pagans. When the Romans—hardly paragons of virtue themselves—encountered Baalism at Carthage, a Phoenician colony, they were utterly grossed out by it.

Literature from this dark culture abounds. A number of years ago, a Syrian peasant accidentally plowed up a flagstone that covered a subterranean passageway leading down into a burial chamber. Subsequent excavations unearthed a large library with inscriptions in various Near Eastern languages, including a new Semitic language now known as Ugaritic. The language was deciphered and the texts were translated. Much of the writing is comprised of erotic poems describing the racy escapades of Baal and his consorts. As a result, we've come to learn more than most of us would ever care to know about the theology and morality of that horrible religion.

The poems are beautifully crafted—yet filled with images and fantasies of a degraded and brutal culture. Without a doubt, Baal worship went hand in hand with appalling violence. Underlying the sophistication of the literature lie tales of murderous rage and frightening cruelty.

In one text, Anat, in a bloody, misanthropic spree, massacres a gathering of male guests whom she invited into her house. After the slaughter she "fastens [their] hands to her girdle"; plunges "knee-deep through their blood; hip-deep through their gore." Then "her liver swells with laughter; her heart swells up with joy."

In another poem, in a wild fit of rage she shouts at her father El:

> *With the might of my [strong] hand*
> > *I will smash your heart;*
> *I will make your gray hair flow with blood;*
> > *The gray hair of your beard with gore.*

And then there's that other aspect of Canaanite culture—one captured in the Old Testament writings as well as in the secular literature of that day: it was awash in sexual aggression and perversion. Some of the poetry is little more than hard-core pornography with an emphasis on lewd sensuality, deviant eroticism, and group sex. Much of it celebrates Baal's potency:

> *Baal makes love to a heifer in Debir*
> > *A young cow in the fields of Shimmat.*
> *He lies with her seventy-seven times—*
> > *Yea, he [copulates] eighty-eight times—*
> *So that she conceives*
> > *And bears a child.*

Myth, in ancient times, gave rise to ritual. The Canaanites acted out their poetry in seasonal ceremonies or cultic dramas, believing these enactments would produce rain and promote fertility. They were dramas with a distinct purpose: They represented a mechanism by which men and women could manipulate the gods.

In the spring, priests and priestesses mated to insure the fertility of soil, beasts, and women. There were more couplings in the fall to express gratitude to the gods, more at the winter solstice to strengthen the fading sun. When it came to conjugation, any old season would do.

Baal worshipers engaged in a catalog of sexual deviancy—polygamy, polyandry, prostitution, adultery, fornication, rape, incest, homosexual partnerships and casual gay encounters, pederasty, and bestiality.

In some instances, the priests of Baal performed the rituals vicariously as representatives of the people, but at other times the people themselves shared in the ritual, participating in all the lusty capers of the priesthood.

Jezebel presided over this cultural revolution, freeing God's children from their moral inhibitions and sexual hang-ups, broadening their minds, stretching their consciences, and justifying every intolerable act in the name of tolerance.

By her teaching, she led Israel into the most venal and corrupt idolatry and sexual immorality. The nation sank deeper and deeper into the shadows and edged nearer and nearer judgment.

But God is never at a loss. He provides for every eventuality. When things look most dark and dangerous, when evil men and women have done their worst, then God can begin. And he usually begins in a very small place by preparing a very obscure person.

Elijah was that person.

Elijah was God's solution to all the evil that Ahab and Jezebel had unleashed in the land.

But what of our day? What of the culture in which you and I find ourselves in the declining days of the second millennium? As Yogi Berra would say, "It's deja vu all over again." The same images that polluted Israel resound in our culture. What terrible times we live in; what awful shame. As Jeremiah said, we've forgotten how to blush (Jeremiah 6:15).

It was Bob Dylan who told us, "The times they are a-changin'."

He was never more right.

Listen to Dartmouth professor Jeffrey Hart, in a recent speech reported by the *Wall Street Journal:*

> A great many things happened all of a sudden in this country in the very recent past. Without going into the right and wrong of every case, I list them objectively. Within living memory, abortion was a felony in virtually every state in the nation. Today abortion is commonplace in America. Demands that it be federally funded are alleged to be rooted in the Constitution.
>
> Within living memory, hard-core pornography was largely kept out of sight, usually by a rough agreement between sellers and authorities. Now the hard-core stuff is available on your newsstand.
>
> Within living memory, school children recited the Pledge of Allegiance every morning, and in many schools simple prayers. At Christmas time, they sang Christmas carols. Suddenly, all of that fell under proscription.
>
> Within living memory, homosexuals were for the most part discreet. Suddenly, we find that they demand public legitimization of their peculiarity, stage parades and demand representation in governing bodies as a legitimate minority. Is there any question that a revolution has in fact been imposed upon an unsuspecting nation?

You have but to look at our culture to realize that it's perishing.

We have broken with our traditional and spiritual past and find ourselves stumbling and lurching into a new Dark

Age of uncertain and bewildering character. There is a growing sense that nothing is true and everything is permitted. "The wicked freely strut about when what is vile is honored among men" (Psalm 12:8).

Evil, morbid influences lead us into ever-deepening confusion—a clutter of distortions, half-truths, bald-faced lies and an addled notion of tolerance that demands we accept everyone's version of truth. There is no final standard; everything varies according to the weather.

G. K. Chesterton once observed that morality, like art, consists of drawing a straight line. Now no one knows where to draw the lines! Once there were boundaries and absolutes. Now, traditional concepts of human sexuality and public decency have warped so radically and thoroughly that *no one knows* what is fine, uplifting, and good.

Who knows what sexual preferences are preferable?

Is teenage sex okay?

Is it good for Heather to have two mommies?

Is Daddy's new roommate okay?

There's no way to heal our confusion, no final authority.

Once we believed in civility and courtesy and compassion. Now we live in an age of cold brutality and insane sexuality where anything goes. We've lost those values and virtues that once prevented us from pandering to our darker instincts.

Raunch, hate, and brutality proliferate. Degraded images and fantasies are pumped into our homes and into the public arena at an astonishing rate, a staple theme of movies, television, and books. Foul-mouthed, mysogynistic "gangsta" rappers talk about dismembering women and "offing" cops. "Hypocrisy, betrayal and greed have unsettled a nation's soul," a *Time* writer observed.

All our doing without God has finally undone us.

Traditional values such as valor, duty, compassion, responsibility, and integrity are considered quaint today. The *Washington Post* noted: "We have reached a state where common decency is no longer common." We've come a long way, baby, but, as the Grateful Dead used to say, "What a long, strange trip it's been." We have pushed ourselves to new levels of personal and social wickedness. All our doing without God has finally undone us.

We are living in what many have described as a post-Christian era. That doesn't mean there are no longer many Christians around; there may in fact be more true believers than ever before. Post-Christian means that *Christian faith no longer plays a role in shaping public opinion and policy.* Christian assumptions and commitments, once widely held, no longer have the presence and impact they formerly had.

When was the last time you attended a theater and heard a dialogue informed by biblical presuppositions? When was the last time you read a book that reflected even remotely the notion that we are unique human beings created in the image of God and dearly loved by him?

Spend a day at Stanford University or the University of California at Berkeley and see if God competes in the war of ideas in either of those arenas. No, he has been marginalized, disappearing from public debate like "the last fading smile of a cosmic Cheshire Cat," as someone has said.

In *The Brothers Karamazov*, Fydor Dostoyevski wrote that "if God does not exist, everything is permissible," which is precisely where we are these days. When God is gone, anything goes; everyone does what is right in his or her own eyes. And when anything goes, "being is beggared," as Emily Dickinson observed. There is no meaning and nothing to live for anymore.

Every true heart feels that emptiness. Underlying a glossy veneer of surface success yawns a black, cavernous void. "What has all our going for the gusto got us?" men and women ask. "Why do we feel so empty and guilty and sad?" Malcolm Muggeridge wrote of our times, "We press on . . . seeking happiness ever more ardently, and finding despair ever more abundantly."

Once again, behind the deceit that informs our culture lies "Sabbathless Satan," working relentlessly to overthrow humanity—to poison our minds and imperil our bodies. Concocting scientific, technical, political, erotic fantasies, he knocks on the door of every heart proclaiming with provoking, cunning voice:

There are no rules . . . Try it once. It won't hurt . . . Why not? Everybody else is doing it . . . Give it up. You're going to give in anyway . . . There are no consequences . . . Go for it. You DESERVE a little pleasure . . . If it feels good, do it . . . C'mon Virginia, why wait? . . . You only go around once—go for the gusto . . . Look out for Number One . . . You shall not die . . . You can be like God!

Satan is a gentleman, Bacon told us, a charming fellow with immense power, subtlety, and thousands of years of experience. His chief aim, of course, is to injure the God against whom he rebels. To accomplish this, Satan misrepresents the Creator to his creatures, always attempting to frustrate his good purposes for them and hopefully—in the process—break the great heart of God. Satan promises us the world, but as Milton said, "All is false and hollow; though his tongue drops manna and makes the worse appear the better reason."

Once again, God is not at a loss.

When things look most perilous and impossible, he is preparing his final solution. You and I are that solution to all the evil that people, principalities, and powers can do. Though you may be only one of teeming millions on this earth and though you may believe you do not count, God says, "You matter and you can make a difference."

That's what this book is about: You can make a difference! So you're not a major player. So you have no political clout or power base. So you're not a Christian quarterback, a converted rock star, a multimedia personality, or a multimillionaire.

You can be a catalyst for change.

You can be used to arrest the spread of corruption in your community.

You can be a source of light in your dark corner of society.

You can be the means by which some part of our crazy world is brought into sync.

We are all designed to be of incalculable use to God.

We are all designed to be of incalculable use to God. He planned our usefulness before time began. "We are God's workmanship," Paul insists, "created in Christ Jesus to do good works, which God prepared in advance for us to do" (Ephesians 2:10).

Perhaps it will be a visible role; more likely it's concealed and hidden. It could be that your entire life will find its meaning in one person whom God wants you to touch in some significant way—or in one event in which he yearns to make himself known.

I do not know what God will do with you and me, but I know this: When we stand before our Lord someday, we will then know that our lives have not been without meaning. "No one is without a divinely appointed task," John Ruskin said, "and the divine means for getting it done."

The Christian world is fascinated nowadays with politics, marketing, management, psychology, and other earthly endeavors, all of which have their proper time and place, but all of which can be nothing more than substitutes for doing things God's way and may amount to little more than puttering. The forces that inveigh against us are not subject to human devices.

The apostle Paul wrote that "our struggle is not against flesh and blood, but against the rulers, against the authorities, against the powers of this dark world and against the spiritual forces of evil in the heavenly realms" (Ephesians 6:12).

The powers of which he speaks are not the strongholds of human evil but the far more insidious and dangerous forces of Satan's underworld.

I recall a message Francis Schaeffer gave in which he envisioned a hypothetical American scientist on an overseas flight who found himself seated next to a rice farmer from a Third World country. During the flight, the two men struck up a conversation and began to quiz one another on their beliefs.

The engineer subscribed to Jesus' teachings—the Sermon on the Mount, no doubt—but he was not a

Christian. He was a humanist and a naturalist. He believed that there is nothing beyond what we can discern with our five senses and that only those things that can be empirically verified are true.

The rice farmer wasn't a Christian either; he was an animist. He believed in an unseen world beyond this one, inhabited by good and evil spirits. Schaeffer asked, "Which of the two is closer to the truth?"

The animist, of course, was thinking more "Christianly" because he believed in the reality of two worlds—one material and one spiritual. He knew that what you see is not what you get, that above and beyond this world is another realm, inhabited by immaterial beings linked to this world and profoundly influencing it.

It does little good to rail and rage against those whom the Devil has cruelly blinded and deceived.

There is simply no such thing as "secular" society. Behind every human power is the power of darkness. Paul says clearly that our struggle is not against human beings but against the spiritual powers that control them. Men and women who embody evil are not the enemy. They are the *victims* of the enemy, "taken . . . captive to do his will" (2 Timothy 2:26). It does little good to rail and rage against those whom the Devil has cruelly blinded and deceived; we must rather do battle with the Devil who has deceived them.

Life is like a Punch and Judy show. When the puppet villain puts in an appearance, we can tongue-lash him and hurl rocks at him or take him out with a club. But what have we accomplished? The man behind the curtain will simply place another puppet on the stage and begin to pull the strings again. Far better to go behind the scenes and take out the puppeteer!

Paul writes, "For though we live in the world, we do not wage war as the world does. The weapons we fight with are not the weapons of the world. On the contrary, they have divine power to demolish [demonic] strongholds" (2 Corinthians 10:3–4).

God has supplied us with the means to get *behind* the puppet-show curtain—to reach behind the scenes. These are not the schemes of human endeavor but the infinitely more powerful strategies of faith: prayer, proclamation, personal righteousness. These are the mechanisms that bring the infinite power of God into play. These are the devices that make a difference.

These are the worst of times and the best of times. Paul put it this way: "[Make] the most of every opportunity, because the days are evil" (Ephesians 5:15).

We read this verse as though Paul is enjoining greater effort because the days are short, but that's not what he's saying at all. He's rather insisting that evil days are days of *opportunity*. The more evil our culture becomes, the more opportunities there will be to put to God's intended use.

A few years ago, I came across an unexpected statement in the Bible—part of Paul's debate with the Athenian philosophers:

From one man he [God] made every nation of men, that they should inhabit the whole earth; and he determined the times set for them and the exact places where they should live. God did this so that men would seek him and perhaps reach out for him and find him, though he is not far from each one of us. "For in him we live and move and have our being." (Acts 17:26–28)

Paul's premise is that God controls human history—permits the rise of nations, determines their geographical boundaries and orchestrates their fall—in order that women and men may reach out for God. History is his story, which he writes for the world's salvation.

Even the forces of evil are used in such a way "that all kingdoms on earth may know that you alone, O LORD, are God" (Isaiah 37:20). God permits wickedness to run its malignant course, allowing (though never condoning) the appearance of the so-called monsters of history—Adolph Hitler, Idi Amin, Nicolae Ceausescu, Saddam Hussein.

The Almighty reins in his power for a time, allowing evil tyrants to make their plays, upsetting men's and women's well-ordered lives, presenting them with dilemmas beyond their ken, shaking what can be shaken so that men and women will seek him and reach out for him and find him. Evil brings pain, but it is the genius of God to bring good out of evil. He works *everything* together for good (Romans 8:28).

Perilous times are times of unparalleled opportunity. Those who know God must not fear them. They should

---

Perilous times are times of unparalleled opportunity.

---

rather buy them up, making the most of every opportunity to show their faith and to share it *because* the days are evil.

"Carpe diem," we say nowadays: "Seize the day." The saying has become so popular and proverbial that most people are surprised when they learn that the phrase has been around for a long time and originated with the old Latin poet Horace:

> *Cut back long hopes. Even as we speak, envious time*
> *Flees: seize the day, trust little in tomorrow.*

Horace was advising a friend not to run out and try to conquer the world but to do the small yet truly significant things that need to be done every day—the duty of the present moment.

"But," you ask, "how will I know when my moment has come? How can I integrate and focus my life on that one duty that God has for me today? The world has a thousand necessities. Issues clamor every day for my attention. What will keep me from being manipulated by every cause and craze?"

God will let you know.

Our usefulness is his business not ours.

"Anyone can find out what will happen," Aslan said to the children as he shook his great mane. "Get up at once and follow me. What will happen? There is only one way of finding out."
—C. S. Lewis, *Prince Caspian*

Seeing Deeper

1. To really understand the conflict between Ahab, Jezebel, and Elijah, you need to get a feel for each personality. With just a few minutes of reading—and a sheet of

paper for notes—you can develop a fascinating profile
of each character.

a. Who was this King Ahab? Describe him from what
you learn in 1 Kings 16:29–33; 18:7–14; 21:1–16, 25–26;
22:30. How would you characterize him?

b. Who was Jezebel? We know the name so well. How
did she earn such a reputation? Read 1 Kings 16:31;
18:4; 19:1–2; 21:7–15, 25; 2 Kings 9:22. How was she
different from Ahab?

c. Who was this Elijah the Tishbite? What do you know
about him from reading 1 Kings 17:1–2, 19–24;
18:21–24, 36–37; 19:1–3; 2 Kings 1:10–15; 2:8.

2. From what you read in this chapter—and what you
recall from other sources—what do you know about
Baalism? What parallels do you see in our culture
today?

3. The author states that "men and women who embody
evil are not the enemy. They are the _____ of the
enemy." What does 2 Timothy 2:24–26 tell us about their
condition? about how to respond to them? How closely
does your view of non-Christians parallel that view
Paul instructed Timothy to take?

4. The author took us to Ephesians 5:16, which says,
"[Make] the most of every opportunity, because the
days are evil" (not, because the days are short). He said,
"Evil days are days of unparalleled opportunity."

Consider the situation Elijah was facing and the real possibility that he would be killed. How could evil days be considered days of opportunity?

Think back to your last time of intense stress (maybe you're in the midst of it right now). In what sense could this time be viewed as God's "day of opportunity" in your life?

*God surrounds himself with incompetents. The people
God uses have rarely been great people, nor have great
people been the people God uses. God looks for misfits and
milquetoasts, shmucks and schlemiels. It's not that he has
to make do with a bunch of fools. He chooses them.*

Chapter Two

Happy to Be Nobody

I'm nobody! Who are you?
Are you—Nobody—Too?
—Emily Dickinson

I clearly recall a day when I dragged myself into the office of the late Ray Stedman, slumped in a chair, and began to bemoan my limitations.

Some months before, I had been handed a ministry of staggering proportions—and knew I didn't have what it took to make it go. In my opinion, I wasn't even close.

"I'm inadequate," I lamented, thinking he would surely replace me.

"Some people labor on all their lives, never knowing they're utterly incompetent."

"Feel inadequate do you?" Ray reflected. "You *are*, my friend—and so am I. It's good that we know it. Some people labor on all their lives, never knowing that they're utterly incompetent."

Talk about incompetence! You would never have guessed that Elijah the Tishbite would amount to much. He was an obscure man from a remote place, far from the more urban and urbane parts of the world.

Elijah hailed from Gilead, on the "other side" of the Jordan River. Wild country. Desolate country. A place of dense forests, deep canyons, vast emptiness, and solitude. The descriptions remind me a great deal of some of the backcountry regions of Idaho, my home state.

He lived in the little town of Tishbe—a community so small it's hard to even locate today. When I think of Tishbe I think of Atlanta, Idaho—a wilderness community founded by Civil War veterans in the 1870s and nestled in a canyon in the Sawtooths at the end of a seventy-mile gravel road. (Every time I drive up there, I have to weld something back on my Jeep.) It's a part of the state people don't know much about. Folks up there live on the edge.

Rugged landforms produce rugged individuals. Elijah was a man for the mountains. He looked the part—fitted out in buckskins and turned-out leather gear. He was a "lord of hair" to use the Hebrew idiom (2 Kings 1:8), which suggests, I suppose, long hair and a lordly beard.

His parents must have been two of the "seven thousand in Israel . . . whose knees [had] not bowed down to Baal and all whose mouths [had] not kissed him" (1 Kings 19:18). Elijah's name, which means "Yahweh is my God," probably reflects that couple's single-minded devotion to the God of Israel.

Elijah was infected by their faith—gripped by an unshakable belief in the reality of the unseen God. For

Elijah, Yahweh was "the LORD, the God of Israel [who] *lives*" (1 Kings 17:1; 18:15, emphasis added). The God of Abraham, Isaac, and Jacob may have been deemed dead in Israel, but the reports of his death had been grossly exaggerated. As far as Elijah was concerned, God was alive and well, the one supreme reality.

Most prophets began their ministries by presenting their credentials, but Elijah had none. He was a modest man with every reason in the world to be modest. God was all he had going for him.

But it was enough, as indeed it is for us.

"Not that we are competent to claim anything for ourselves," Paul writes, "but our competence comes from God. *He* has made us competent" (2 Corinthians 3:5–6, emphasis added).

We think of the prophets as fierce, determined zealots with flinty faces and flaming eyes. They had no ambiguities, no uncertainties, nothing to distract them from their awesome task of setting a warped world right. But God rarely begins with such enthusiasts. He almost always starts with women and men who know their limitations.

God fears our ability—and so should we. Powerful people are bothersome, rushing about in their own strength, overly optimistic about their abilities, disgustingly fearless, invincible and all-knowing, blatantly self-generating, and generally blundering around and getting in God's way. As Jesus put it, "The flesh [human effort] counts for nothing" (John 6:63).

Men and women who work the works of God are those who realize the impossibility of God ever using them. Paul's succinct philosophy of life, "We are weak," is not pious palaver; it's a humbling fact.

God surrounds himself with incompetents. The people God uses have rarely been great people, nor have great people been the people God uses. Nietzche looked for a "a strong kind of man, most highly gifted in intellect and will." God looks for misfits and milquetoasts, shmucks and schlemiels.

It's not that he has to make do with a bunch of fools. He *chooses* them.

Listen to Paul:

Brothers, think of what you were when you were called. Not many of you were wise by human standards; not many were influential; not many were of noble birth. But God chose the foolish things of the world to shame the wise; God chose the weak things of the world to shame the strong. He chose the lowly things of this world and the despised things—and the things that are not—to nullify the things that are, so that no one may boast before him. It is because of him that you are in Christ Jesus, who has become for us wisdom from God—that is, our righteousness, holiness and redemption. Therefore, as it is written: "Let him who boasts boast in the Lord." (1 Corinthians 1:26–31)

Few of us have clout. We're neither superstars nor supersaints. But therein lies our strength.

Oh, to be sure, some of God's children are rich and famous. But frankly, not many. (Lady Hamilton, a member of the British noble family, once quipped that she was saved by the letter *M*, for, as she put it, "Paul said 'not *many* are called.' He did not say 'not *any*.' ") Most of us are ordinary people, unimportant, insignificant, and unnecessary in the eyes of the world. Few of us have clout. We're neither superstars nor supersaints. Like Saint Francis's "Jugglers," we are the joke that God is playing on the world.

But therein lies our strength.

It is awareness of weakness that keeps us strong enough to never be weak.

Paul, who was inclined toward paradoxes, put it this way: "When I am weak, then I am strong" (2 Corinthians 12:10). For Milton's Satan, "to be weak is to be miserable"; for Paul, to be weak is to be strong. It is awareness of that weakness that keeps us strong enough to never be weak.

"If I must boast," Paul wrote, "I will boast of the things that show my weakness. The God and Father of the Lord Jesus, who is to be praised forever, knows that I am not lying. In Damascus the governor under King Aretas had the city of the Damascenes guarded in order to arrest me. But I was lowered in a basket from a window in the wall and slipped through his hands" (2 Corinthians 11:30–33).

Paul came to Damascus thinking he was God's gift to his generation—perfectly suited to evangelize the Jews. He had reason to be confident: "circumcised on the eighth day, of the people of Israel, of the tribe of Benjamin, a Hebrew of Hebrews; in regard to the law, a Pharisee; as for zeal, persecuting the church; as for legalistic righteousness, faultless" (Philippians 3:5–6). He was an Israelite indeed. He was the little engine that could!

And so he tackled the thing that couldn't be done—and he couldn't do it.

Instead of a revival, he precipitated a riot.

The Christians in Damascus put him in a foul and stinking fish basket, lowered him over the wall, and sent him away, pleading with him not to return lest he undo all that God had been doing.

What a bitter embarrassment! It was the worst day of Paul's life—*and the best*. That's the day he learned that he was, as he later put it, "nothing" (2 Corinthians 12:11).

But not to worry! In time Paul became "somebody." He rounded out the picture this way: "But we have this treasure [deity] in jars of clay [humanity] to show that this all-surpassing power is from God and not from us" (2 Corinthians 4:7).

Deity in humanity—God in a jar. Paul carried about in his own body the presence and essence of *God*.

It comes to this: Every natural virtue, every endearing quality, every proclivity toward goodness comes from God. Without him we can do nothing. We must accept our limits—no, we must *love* them. They are God's gift to us. It is the way we are.

Nothing in us is a source of hope.

Nothing in us is worth defending.

Nothing in us is special and worth admiring.

When we accept that fact, we can rest in him who alone is wisdom, righteousness, and power.

Consider Moses, once part of Egypt's aristocracy, educated and finished in the best Egyptian schools, competent and adequate for anything. Yet after forty years of exile on the backside of the desert, he was good for nothing. Once a man of great strength and resolve, he had been ground down and diminished until he had nothing left to give. He was kaput, done for, out of order. In other words, he was just about to the point where God could actually use him.

One day, near Mount Sinai, Moses saw a bush ablaze and went off to investigate. Clearly this was no ordinary bush, for though it burned it was not burned up! "Moses thought, 'I will go over and see this strange sight—why the bush does not burn up.' When the LORD saw that he had gone over to look, God called to him from within the bush, 'Moses, Moses!' And Moses said, 'Here I am' " (Exodus 3:3–4).

God spoke out of the bush: "I have come down to rescue [my people] from the hand of the Egyptians and to bring them up out of that land into a good and spacious land. . . . The cry of the Israelites has reached me, and I have seen the way the Egyptians are oppressing them. So now, go. I am sending you to Pharaoh to bring my people the Israelites out of Egypt" (verses 8–10).

Forty years before, Moses would have accepted the task with eagerness. Now he was full of doubt and disclaimer: *"Who am I* that I should go to Pharaoh and bring the Israelites out of Egypt?" (verse 11, emphasis added). Moses didn't know who he was. Disappointment, failure, the wild loneliness of the desert, and the utter silence of God had devastated his ego.

God's way of reestablishing Moses' sense of worth, unlike our way, was not to list his assets and abilities. Instead God reminded Moses of his presence: "I will be *with* you!" he said (verse 12, emphasis added).

That's always God's answer to our lack of identity and our sense of inadequacy. It doesn't matter who we are. What matters is that God dwells *with* us. "I am with you" is the answer to all our deficiencies.

And then there was Gideon, the ineffectual little man who described himself as the "least" in his household (Judges 6:15). The word means trifling, or small. Gideon was another nobody.

For seven years Israel had endured the humiliation of periodic raids as waves of Bedouin on camels had swept across the countryside, raping, pillaging, and ruining what they could not carry away. "Midian so impoverished the Israelites that they cried out to the LORD for help" (Judges 6:6).

God heard their prayers and sent help: The Angel of the Lord—the Lord representing himself in the form of an angel—appeared to Gideon as he was hiding in a winepress, hunched down in a hollow in the rocks, beating out wheat with a stick, improvising to save his grain crop from the marauding Midianites.

The angel said to Gideon, "The LORD is with you, mighty warrior" (verse 12), using an expression that denotes a member of the military aristocracy.

Gideon missed the irony in the angel's greeting and launched into a bitter tirade against God: "If the LORD is with us, why has all this happened to us? Where are all his wonders that our fathers told us about when they said, 'Did not the LORD bring us up out of Egypt?' But now the LORD has abandoned us and put us into the hand of Midian" (verse 13).

"The LORD is with you." Where was the Lord when they murdered my brothers? (see Judges 8:18–21). Where indeed were all his "wonders"? God in the hands of an angry sinner!

The Lord shrugged off Gideon's assault and said, "Go in the strength you have and save Israel out of Midian's hand" (6:14). Literally, "Go in *this* your strength."

What strength?

Gideon had none.

Exactly!

The secret of Gideon's strength was his weakness. God said, "I will be with you, and you will strike down all the Midianites together" (verse 16). Look for me in every time of need.

Our human reaction to any difficult assignment is to say "I can't!" That's perfectly natural. But then God says, "My grace is sufficient for you; go in this your strength."

At that moment, "I can't" becomes blasphemy.

God has promised to meet every need we have, but he cannot do it until we admit our need and cast ourselves on him. When we have done this, we don't have to worry about whether he will find us fit enough to do his work. In the words of the old hymn, "All the fitness he requireth is to feel our need of him."

Listen to Jeremiah's complaint:

"Ah Sovereign LORD," I said, "I do not know how to speak; I am only a child."

But the Lord said to me, "Do not say, 'I am only a child.' You must go to everyone I send you to and say whatever I command you. Do not be afraid of them, for I am with you and will rescue you," declares the LORD.

Then the LORD reached out his hand and touched my mouth and said to me, "Now, I have put my words in your mouth."
(Jeremiah 1:6–9)

Jeremiah, like Elijah, was called to kingdom service at a critical time. The days were evil. Judah's leaders were playing politics, ignoring God's offer of help, disregarding the ominous signs, forgetting that God is faithful to his threats as well as to his promises. Jeremiah, a callow youth, was called for such an hour.

We should never say to God, "I can't do that" because we're too young or too inexperienced. Youth and inexperience are never a problem to God. Most of the biblical people God pressed into service were undeveloped: Jeremiah was a mere slip of a boy; the disciples were green and untested; even Jesus, from the standpoint of an old grizzly like me, was much too young to save the world. No, youthfulness never frustrates God. Only immaturity does, and immaturity can be outgrown by the grace of God.

Nor should we ever say no to God because we are afraid. Listen—we're *all* afraid. Whoever first said, "We have nothing to fear but fear," was dead wrong. It's the absence of fear that we should fear. We should always be afraid, a sentiment a friend of mine refers to as the "chicken factor."

Jacob and Wilhelm Grimm tell a fairy tale about a young man who was normal in every respect except he could not shudder. All sorts of shocks were prepared for him—ghosts, hanged men, devil-cats, and bodies in coffins—but to no avail. He was hampered by his absence of fear.

Fear is the natural human reaction to any difficult or dangerous undertaking, and God does not condemn it. But he does not want us to be dominated by fear. Jesus' consistent word to his disciples was "Don't be afraid," using a verb tense that suggests continuance: "Don't *keep on* fearing." We need not be intimidated by our fear or overcome by it, for God can turn our fear into strength.

God calls us to get a grip on him and walk through the walls of our fear.

God calls us to get a grip on him and by his power walk through the walls of our fear. Courage is mastery of fear, not absence of fear. We should resist our fear—meet it with faith. Jesus has said, "I am with you always, to the very end of the age" (Matthew 28:20).

Nor should we worry about our impediments and afflictions. None are so severe that God cannot use them. Moses said, on the occasion of his call, "O Lord, I have never been eloquent, neither in the past nor since you have spoken to your servant. I am slow of speech and tongue."

The language suggests that Moses had a serious speech impediment: perhaps he stuttered. "The Lord said to him, 'Who gave man his mouth? Who makes him deaf or mute? Who gives him sight or makes him blind? Is it not I, the LORD? Now go; I will help you speak and will teach you what to say' " (Exodus 4:11–12).

Our impairments, disabilities, and handicaps are not accidents. They are God-designed. He creates every one of our flaws for his own good.

Years ago in a class at the University of California in Berkeley, we were handed a small tablet containing a crude Canaanite inscription. It was a prayer to Baal. It read something like this: "Oh, Baal, cut through the impediment of my tongue." I couldn't help but reflect on that miserable man or woman who left this sacrifice and pled with the idol for release. Then I thought of Moses and of God's way of dealing with his affliction—not to remove it but to endow it with strength and utilize it for good.

Paul said of his handicap: "Three times I pleaded with the Lord to take it away from me. But he said to me, 'My grace is sufficient for you, for my power is made perfect in weakness.' Therefore," Paul concluded, "I will boast all the more gladly about my weaknesses, so that Christ's power may rest on me. That is why, for Christ's sake, I delight in weaknesses. . . . For when I am weak, then I am strong" (2 Corinthians 12:8–10).

And so it comes to this: We should never worry about ourselves—our voice, our looks, our personalities, our educations, our intelligence. God sets aside conventional notions of maturity, adequacy, and efficiency and looks for those who know their limitations. The Lord assures us, "This is the one I esteem: he who is humble and contrite in spirit, and trembles at my word" (Isaiah 66:2).

The realization that we are weak and powerless is the beginning of God's work.

From weakness we are made strong. The realization that we are weak and powerless is the beginning of God's work.

We must, "confess ourselves poor creatures," George MacDonald said, "for that is the beginning of being great. To try to persuade ourselves that we are something when we are nothing is terrible loss; to confess that we are nothing is to lay the foundation of being something."

This is the life: living without apparent power, prosperity, or adequacy, wholly dependent on God, available to him to be put to his intended use.

We don't have to render the Big Answer.
We don't have to perform the Immortal Deed.
We don't have to be Sensational or Remarkable.
All we need is God.

My Father, I commend myself to you, I give myself to you, I leave myself in your hands. My Father, do with me as you wish. Whatever you do with me, I thank you, I accept everything. I am ready for anything. I thank you always. So long as your will is done in me . . . I have no other wish, my God. I put my soul into your hands, giving it to you, my God, with all my heart's love, which makes me crave to abandon myself to you without reserve, with utter confidence. For are you not my Father?

—From *Meditations of a Hermit* by Charles de Foucauld

Seeing Deeper

1. Read 1 Kings 16:29–33 and 18:2–4. Describe what life must have been like in Israel in those days. How might you have felt if you lived there?

2. We think of the prophets as fierce, determined zealots with flinty faces and flaming eyes. But what does Scripture show us? Read these verses and you may be surprised.

　　a. Exodus 4:10–13

　　b. Judges 6:15

　　c. 1 Kings 19:3–4

　　d. 1 Corinthians 2:1–3

3. The author states: "The realization that we are weak and powerless is the beginning of God's work." Yes, but—how are we to have the confidence to step out in the name of the Lord if we must begin by believing ourselves incompetent and inadequate for the task?

4. We're quick to praise someone for a job well done or a talent well expressed. As a recipient of such praise, how can you respond appropriately in the light of the following verses?

　　a. 1 Corinthians 4:7

　　b. Luke 17:7–10

　　c. Isaiah 66:2

5. If we're going to be responsible for God's work, we tend to believe we need to be strong and especially gifted or equipped for the task. What's wrong with that assumption in light of:

　　a. Exodus 3:8–10. Note who's to do what.

　　b. 2 Corinthians 3:5. What expectation is placed on us?

　　c. 2 Corinthians 4:7. What's said about our strength?

6. Haven't we all prayed "God change me so I'll be able to . . . ?" In other words, make me different than I am so I'll be capable of doing something significant for you.

   a. Read Exodus 4:10 again. What was Moses' problem? Did God change it?

   b. Read 2 Corinthians 12:7–9. What was Paul's problem? Did God change it?

   c. In both cases, what did God offer *instead?* Does this insight have potential for changing how you feel about your own limitations? about your openness to new ministry?

We can never know in prospect what God will do with us—his will is always best seen in retrospect—but when the time comes to know we will know. I cannot tell you how you will know but you will know. Life gets exciting when we give God permission to chart the course. He takes us where others have never gone before and where we've never thought we could go. He leads us beyond anything we could ever ask or think, beyond our wildest dreams. He takes the smallest events and turns them into momentous occasions.

Chapter Three

The Power of Prevailing Prayer

I asked for words!
Life led me to a wood,
Set me in solitude
Where speech is still and
Wisdom comes by prayer.
—Chester B. Emerson

Travelers brought snatches of news from Samaria. Messenger after messenger told how Jezebel had torn down Yahweh's altars and replaced them with the bloody, licentious rites of the Baals. Elijah's heart flamed with indignation at these reports. He was "very zealous for the LORD God Almighty" (1 Kings 19:10), but what could he do? He was only one person, far from the centers of power and control.

According to James, Elijah did the only thing he could to do under the circumstances. He prayed.

Elijah was a man just like us. He prayed earnestly that it would not rain, and it did not rain on the land for three and a half years. (James 5:17)

Apparently, the most important thing about prayer is sticking to it.

Elijah prayed *earnestly*. To use James's precise phrase, "Elijah prayed with prayer," an idiom that suggests dogged perseverance. Apparently, the most important thing about prayer is sticking to it.

Jesus said, we "should always pray and not give up" and then told a story about a tenacious widow who kept pressing an unscrupulous judge to hear her case. The judge flatly refused to grant her a hearing—at first. There was nothing in it for him. But the widow would not be put off. She kept persisting until the exasperated magistrate finally gave in (Luke 18:1–8).

On another occasion, Jesus pictured prevailing prayer as a man pounding on a friend's door at midnight to borrow a loaf of bread. The rudely awakened householder tried to send his audacious friend away, but like the persistent widow, the man refused to be dismissed. He kept knocking and knocking and *knocking*—until he eventually got what he wanted (11:5–8).

This is not to say God bears any resemblance to that indisposed friend or disinclined judge. Not at all. Jesus is arguing from the lesser to the greater. If *even* a reluctant friend or an irascible, unwilling judge will sooner or later relent and give what someone keeps on asking, *how much more* will a loving, caring Father give his own children what they ask?

"Will not God bring about justice for his chosen ones, who cry out to him day and night? Will he keep putting them off? If tell you, he will see that they get justice, and quickly" (18:7–8).

"Quickly," of course, is a relative term.

God's day can add up to a thousand years. He's rarely in a hurry, but neither does he delay. He just does what he's decided to do when he has decided to do it.

The early church fathers talked about "a holy leisure," by which they meant a slow, unhurried pace of life tuned to God's rhythm and cadence. It's a matter of slowing oneself down and staying in step with him, praying, waiting, listening. God's answer will always come in time.

Jesus said, "Ask and it will be given to you; seek and you will find; knock and the door will be opened to you" (Matthew 7:7). We must keep on beating a path to his door, asking, seeking, knocking on his heart of hearts until he replies. "For everyone who asks receives; he who seeks finds; and to him who knocks, the door will be opened" (verse 8).

Paul commands us, "I urge, then, first of all, that requests, prayers, intercession and thanksgiving be made for everyone" (1 Timothy 2:1). By "first of all," Paul means "of primary importance."

Prayer is the main thing—the center, the core, the root, the spirit of all we do. It is our primary task.

In reality, no one has to tell us to pray. Prayer springs from us impulsively and instinctively in the face of over-whelming necessity. When we're pushed beyond our limits . . . frightened out of our wits . . . pressed out of our comfort zones . . . propelled along a white-water torrent of change—we resort to prayer as if by reflex. "The natural thing," MacDonald said, "is straight to the Father's knee."

But we must realize that we are *always* needy people—inadequate, deficient, desperately dependent on God. Without him we can do *nothing*. Prayer is the highest expression of that dependence.

Perhaps the most startling of all Jesus' statements about himself was his insistence that he too was a dependent being, sustained alone by prayer. "By myself I can do *nothing*" (John 5:30, emphasis added).

Jesus' humiliation included taking on our weakness and our ignorance. He had no wisdom of his own, no power, no righteousness. He, like us, had to rely on God every moment of every day. Each morning he had to abandon his own strength and strategies and offer himself up, confident that his Father's power would lead him into greater works than he could ever envision or accomplish alone. "Oh the mystery of humility," F. B. Meyer said, "that he who planned all things should live a life of such absolute dependence."

Prayer, for Jesus, was an expression of deeply felt need. It was the environment in which he lived, the air he breathed. Subject to constant interruption, busy beyond comparison, jostled by friends and foes, hassled and harried, he managed to keep up his communion with God. Every situation was an occasion for prayer.

When he held in his hands the small pieces of bread and saw the vast multitude to be fed, he prayed. When he faced the death of his friend at Bethany, he called on his Father's name. When certain Greeks came seeking him, he asked the Father to glorify his name. Jesus' life was continuous prayer, triggered by continuous need.

We too must be "faithful in prayer" (Romans 12:12), or as Paul wrote in another place, we must "pray continually" (1 Thessalonians 5:17).

Describing his understanding of these verses, Civil War general Stonewall Jackson said, "I never seal a letter without putting a word of prayer under the seal. I never receive a dispatch from the post without a brief sending of my thoughts upward. I never meet my troops without a moment's petition on those who go out and those who come in. Everything calls me to prayer."

The saints of medieval days saw in everything a summons to prayer: the tolling of a bell, the flight of a swallow, the fall of a leaf. For myself the best reminders are the people I meet:

- the harried young woman who waits on me in a restaurant
- the blasé secretary who greets me in an office
- the weary old man who lives next door

All are reminders of the deep needs that lie all around me and that I cannot meet. All are incentives to prayer. I can do nothing for these men and women, but God can. I can pray for them silently as I encounter them, and ask God to use me or another instrument to make visible the invisible Christ.

That perspective makes life a matter of prevailing prayer, so much a part of us that we can say as David said, "I *am* prayer" (Psalm 109:4. Most translations supply "I am *a man of* prayer," but the text reads simply, "I am prayer"). Prayer is our essence and genius—our principal work and the means by which everything else is done.

Fitting In

Prayer is worship. Our praying should be full of adoration, affection, and fondness for God. It is one of the best ways in the world to love him.

Prayer is petition. We can ask for anything—even the most difficult things—and know that God hears us. MacDonald said, "Anything big enough to occupy our minds is big enough to hang a prayer on."

Prayer is asking for understanding. It is the means by which we comprehend what God is saying to us in his Word.

Prayer moves what we know from our heads to our hearts; it's our hedge against hypocrisy, the way by which we ring true.

Prayer focuses us and unites our fragmented hearts. We have a thousand necessities. It's impossible for us to simplify them and integrate them into one. We should pray with David, "Give me an *undivided* heart" (Psalm 86:11, emphasis added).

Prayer is all these things but it is more: *it is the means by which we fit in*. It is the way God aligns us with him and enables us to collaborate with him in complete union and oneness. Seen in that way, prayer is more like *listening* than anything else—being quiet in God's presence, waiting on God until we know what to do. "If you pray the work," Mother Teresa said, "you will know what to do."

Paul wrote:

> *We do not know what we ought to pray for, but the Spirit himself intercedes for us with groans that words cannot express. And he who searches our hearts knows the mind of the Spirit, because*

the Spirit intercedes for the saints in accordance with God's will.
(Romans 8:26–27)

As we pray the Spirit of God directs our thoughts.

We come with a list of petitions; he gently leads us from our list to his.

We set out to express one concern; he interjects another.

In the hours of waiting on him, he sorts out our misunderstandings, dispels our confusion, and shows us how he wants us to pray and what he wants us to do.

Prayer is the best cure for our confusion.

Prayer, then, is the best cure for our confusion. If in your perplexity and worry you find yourself without a clue, present yourself before God in stillness of heart and ask him to create prayers, supplications, and intercessions within you. The best prayers are initiated by God. What he creates is worth far more than anything you or I could ever say.

As Elijah pondered his nation's terrible betrayal and steeped his soul in prayer, his thoughts began to reflect God's thoughts. He recalled the words of one of his prophets:

Beware, lest your [Israel's] hearts be deceived and you turn away and serve other gods and worship them. Or the anger of the LORD will be kindled against you, and He will shut up the heavens so that there will be no rain and the ground will not yield its fruit; and you will perish quickly from the good land which the LORD is giving you. (Deuteronomy 11:16–17 NASB)

Elijah contemplated Moses' terrible threat. He considered its implications. And as he pondered and prayed, the light suddenly broke through and he realized what God intended to do: It was his plan to correct his people through drought and famine. And so Elijah began to pray according to God's will "earnestly that it would not rain" (James 5:17).

Then, as he continued to pray, Elijah learned what God wanted *him* to do: he was to present himself before Ahab and Jezebel and announce God's judgment on the nation.

It will be different for you and me.

God is utterly unpredictable. Surprise and serendipity are always on his mind.

It was Joaquin Andujar, pitcher and poet for the St. Louis Cardinals, who said you could sum up baseball in one word: "You never know." His word count was off, but he captured the quintessence of baseball and of God. The only thing predictable about God is that he is utterly unpredictable. Surprise and serendipity are always on his mind. "Wisdom should always reckon on the unforeseen."

I don't know what God will do with you and me. But he knows. Our task is to pray and to wait on him until he puts us to his intended use. It's up to him to get us to the right place at the right time.

That means that we must hold our plans loosely, giving God the right to revise them or replace them entirely, permitting him to advise, correct, and prompt us. We can never know in prospect what God will do with us—his will is always best seen in retrospect—but when the time comes to know, we will know. I cannot tell you how you will know, but you will know. "God will show you," MacDonald said, "Do not fear the how."

Life gets exciting when we give God permission to chart the course. He takes us where others have never gone before and where we've never thought we could go. He leads us beyond anything we could ever ask or think, beyond our wildest dreams. He takes the smallest events and turns them into momentous occasions.

Take Jesus' disciple Andrew.

Andrew, you may remember, led his brother Simon Peter to Jesus (John 1:42). As far as we know, that's the only person he managed to win. But what a conversion! That one convert affected thousands through his words on the day of Pentecost—and went on to evangelize thousands more. He's still reaching millions through his written word.

Paul, "compelled by the Spirit," went to Jerusalem and touched off a riot that took him to Caesarea and then to Rome for trial. While under house arrest there, Paul was chained to members of Caesar's Praetorian Guard, the choice young men of the empire who, after serving in the palace guard, became members of the Roman aristocracy. They were the mind movers and kingmakers of the empire. These fine young men were with the apostle in four-hour shifts, looking over his shoulder as he penned his epistles, listening as he boldly "preached the kingdom of God and taught about the Lord Jesus Christ" (Acts 28:31). Paul's pregnant greeting to Philippi from "those who belong to Caesar's household" (Philippians 4:22), suggests that some of these young men had become members of the household of faith and were taking the gospel back to the barracks. Though confined, Paul was moving the heart of the Roman Empire.

"I want you to know, brothers," Paul wrote, "that what has happened to me has really served to advance the gospel" (Philippians 1:12). Who could have premeditated or planned such a course?

There was that Samaritan woman whom Jesus "happened" to meet at the well. She was seeking God; he was seeking her (John 4:23). Our Lord was there to make the connection. "She came forth sinning; she went back winning thousands to the water that was not from the well."

"Many of the Samaritans from that town believed in him because of the woman's testimony" (John 4:39).

And then there was that demonized Gerasene whom Jesus delivered from the legion (Mark 5:1–20). You know the story: how the man pled to be delivered from his terrible conglomeration of evil spirits; how Jesus exorcised the demons and cast them into a herd of nearby swine.

The man, emancipated, asked to accompany Jesus but was told: "'Go home to your family and tell them how much the Lord has done for you, and how he has had mercy on you.' So the man went away and began to tell in the Decapolis how much Jesus had done for him."

The world has yet to see what God will do through you and me.

Turned loose on an unsuspecting population, he went throughout the region celebrating his cure and turning the countryside upside down. When Jesus returned to that region, many sought to be saved. Whole cities were renewed by the witness of one reclaimed soul.

The world has yet to see what God will do through you and me.

Our task is to pray and wait and see what that will be. God will not allow you to waste your life. He will tell you what to do, and he will see to it that you bear fruit for him.

God will not allow you to waste your life. He wills that you bear fruit for him.

We're not called upon to originate, initiate, make far-reaching plans, or execute them but rather by the power of prayer to put ourselves into God's hands. "So shall you build to good and lasting purpose," Meyer said.

Some years ago, Carolyn, my wife, and I came across one of the Lord's choice servants, Grahame Nicolson, serving in a small place in Montana with powerful effect. He shared a poem with us, written by his father and given to him on the day he left home. Each time I read it, I'm touched by the words.

> *Go, then, my son;*
> *And may God give you*
> *To taste deeply of his matchless love and grace.*
> *And in that glorious work on Calvary's cross begun,*
> *May you, for Him, secure an honored place.*
>
> *It may not always be the garden of the Lord—*
> *Not every tree a glorious fruit will bear.*
> *But just remember*
> *Neath the barren soil, there are the roots*

> *Which by the power of prayer,*
> *Will spring to life*
> *And glorify our God.*
>
> —Carl C. Nicolson

Seeing Deeper

1. "In reality, no one has to tell us to pray. Prayer springs from us . . . instinctively." It's part of that God-given knowledge we all have deep inside that tells us he exists. Even the atheist prays when in danger. But *effective* prayer is something more. What are some of the elements of effective prayer?

2. Jesus said we should "pray and not give up" (Luke 18:1). Read Luke 11:1–13. What is the value of persistence?

3. "Prayer is the main thing . . . our primary task." When there's so much to *do,* how can prayer be our primary task? Honestly evaluating your own list of tasks, where does prayer usually rank in that list? Number 1? Number 3? Number 33? Why do you think you prioritize it the way you do?

4. "Prayer is the highest expression of our dependence on God. [Jesus] too was a dependent being." Isn't that amazing? We often begin an enterprise with prayer, then move out to do our best, vaguely hoping for God's continued blessing. But Jesus not only began with

prayer, he prayed repeatedly as he encountered needs in daily life.

Turn to Philippians 4:6 and 1 Thessalonians 5:17. How can we remind ourselves of our continual need to depend on God?

5. "Prayer is many things."

a. "It is worship." What is worship? Do you worship when you pray?

b. "Prayer is petition." We all know what petition is. That's what we do best! But as we petition, what should we keep in mind? See Matthew 7:7–11 and Philippians 4:6.

c. "Prayer is asking for understanding." See James 1:5. Do you pray for spiritual understanding? Is your life changed as a result? What's your frustration level when you find yourself *not* understanding?

d. "Prayer focuses us," and is the only "cure for confusion." How does prayer help you to become focused? How does the Lord help you sort through confusing issues and circumstances?

e. "Prayer . . . aligns us with him. . . . Prayer is more like listening." Turn to Jeremiah 42:3. Do you ever think of prayer as listening? How can prayer become a way for you to listen to God more carefully?

God's word requires little or no ornamentation. It simply needs to be stated. Truth sets up a sympathetic vibration in the soul. God's law is written there, which means that everything we say has been heard before. When we speak truth the conscience resonates with it. The hardest heart is at the mercy of God's word.

Chapter Four

The Word That Moves the World

I did nothing. The Word did it all.
I simply taught, preached, wrote God's Word,
otherwise I did nothing.
And while I slept and drank Wittenberg beer
with Philipp and Amsdorf, the Word
weakened all who opposed me.

—Martin Luther
on the Protestant Reformation

It was all very sudden.

Like the Ancient Mariner who seized the wedding guests and made them listen to an uglier tale than they wanted to hear, Elijah appeared abruptly and uttered his awesome line.

As the LORD, the God of Israel, lives, whom I serve, there will
be neither dew nor rain in the next few years except at my word.
(1 Kings 17:1)

Aleksandr Solzhenitsyn has reminded us that just as a shout in the mountains can start an avalanche, so a single word, spoken in God's way and in his time, can have a seismic effect. Elijah's brief sentence, uttered with clarity and passion, triggered the landslide that swept the ground from under his opponents and jolted Israel into remembering the God of her fathers.

Here was a bumpkin—unkempt, unpolished, uneducated, unaccustomed to the manners and ways of the court—a man weak where we are weak, tempted where we are tempted. This simple man from the wrong side of the Jordan stood alone in the polished halls of the cultured and powerful. Flanked by symbols of earthly might and in the presence of one of the most influential men in the Middle East at the time, he was not silenced by the one or the other. Surely frightened out of his wits, he remained conscious of a greater power: the power of the Word of God!

We must never rest until we have Elijah's confidence. Then God can work again through us the wonders and marvels of days gone by.

The ancient rabbis contrived a lengthy conversation in which Elijah tried to convince Ahab of his wrongdoing, but I think Elijah's message was necessarily terse. More words would not have made any difference. Yogi Berra observed, "There are some people who, if they don't know, you can't tell them." Ahab had to find out for himself that God's Word was true.

In due time the saying came to pass. It quit raining. And it didn't rain for three and a half years. Josephus, the Jewish historian, reports that the Greek writer Menander "mentioned this drought in his account of the acts of Ethbaal, king of the Tyrians; where he says thus, 'Under him was want of rain' " (*Antiquities* 8.13.2). In the ancient Near East, and in Canaan in particular, everything was related to rain and the progression and alternation of the seasons. Summer was a period of drought and sterility. The springs and intermittent streams ceased, and only large rivers such as the Jordan continued to flow. During this dry period, there was almost no rainfall. Unless the crops were near a source of running water, they had to be irrigated from wells and cisterns, sources dependent on reserves stored during the rainy season.

In the mythology of the times, Canaanites depicted the alternations in nature as violent and lusty conflict among the gods. The representations of Baal normally depicted him brandishing a club in one hand, symbolizing thunder, and a stylized lightening bolt in the other. On his head he wore a helmet with horns suggesting his association with the bull, a symbol of fertility and potency.

Baal was the storm god who drove the clouds across the sky and let his voice be heard in the crash of thunder. In violent conflict he drove off Mot, the god of the dry season, and brought rain and fertility to the land. Baal determined when the rain would fall. As a Canaanite poet wrote:

> *Lo, it is the time of his rain;*
> *Baal sets the season,*
> *And gives forth his voice in the clouds.*
> *He flashes lightning to the earth.*

Mot, whose name means "death," was the god of drought and sterility. He presided over the dry season and appeared in Canaanite mythology as Baal's chief antagonist. When Mot came, Baal's time was over and he had to pass from the scene. He was ordered to take everything connected with fertility into the depths of the earth. As he descended into the earth, the season of drought arrived and the rain and clouds vanished; the streams dried up and the vegetation languished. Baal's worshipers cried out,

> *Where is Baal, the Overcomer?*
> *Where is the Prince, the Lord of the earth?*

In time he was found, brought to life, and once more installed as king on Mount Sapan in the North. Baal' had overcome! The rains returned; fertility was assured. His worshipers praised him:

> *Our king is Baal, the Overcomer;*
> *Our Judge, and no one is above him!*

Baal, of course, was nothing more than a myth, a superstitious patchwork of traditions, old legends, and outright lies. He was a construct, a virtual reality created out of nothing, a gigantic hoax.

But behind the myth and fakery . . . behind the rituals and rites . . . behind the chanting and hollow traditions— was a monstrous reality—a great seething evil.

An invisible power was insidiously subverting the minds of women and men, girls and boys, and taking away their souls—"a mighty hunter and his prey was man."

So it is today: something wicked this way comes. There is a barbarous and murderous personality behind all the lies that clutter the media and cloud our minds. He's the one of whom Jesus said, "He was a murderer from the beginning, not holding to the truth, for there is no truth in him. When he lies, he speaks his native language, for he is a liar and the father of lies" (John 8:44).

We live in world of cosmic deceit, hidden agendas, treacherous motivations, illusions, and lies. And Satan is behind it all. His strategy is to deceive. His objective is to destroy. His shrewd, cruel mind is behind the lies that buffet us all day long, the media messages that encourage us to "find ourselves" in something or someone other than the living God, to go for all the gusto, but to leave our Savior out.

The lie comes into the world in the guise of beauty and good (our minds are repelled by ugliness and obvious evil), but the deceit inevitably sickens the soul and it begins to die, for when Satan has accomplished his purpose and separated men and women from God, what can they do but wither and die?

Denis deRougement in a book entitled *The Devil's Share* makes the following comment:

> There are two ways of lying, as there are two ways of deceiving a customer. If the scale registers 15 ounces, you can say, "It is a pound." Your lie will remain relative to an invariable measure of the true. If the customer checks it he can see that he is being robbed, and he knows by how much you are robbing him; a truth remains as a judge between you. But if you tamper with the scale itself, it is the criterion of the truth which is denatured; there is no longer any possible control. And little by little you will forget that you are cheating. You may even bet that you will exercise all your scruples in giving exact weight, perhaps by adding a few pinches for "good measure," for the smile of the buyer and the satisfaction of

your virtue. That is "pure" lying, the moment you falsify the
scale of truth itself, all your virtues are at the service of evil
and are accomplices in its contagion.

When the standard is corrupted, even the honorable
become the agents of evil. They will believe they are doing
right when in fact what they are doing is dead wrong, and
they will unwittingly foist their wrongdoing on others.

That's what has happened today. Satan has moved the
parameters so that even principled people have been
brought into the service of evil. Their lack of fixed reference
points has led them into profound moral confusion and a
deep sense of insecurity.

In a cartoon depicting two people talking, one said to
the other, "I believe in evil. I just don't know what *qualifies*."
People still believe in good and evil, it's just that hardly
anyone knows where the parameters are—an agnosticism
that makes for a very dangerous and uncertain world.

We are like children in these matters: we long for the
safety of a moral framework. It's unnatural to exist without
benchmarks and reference points, and unnerving, like the
sensations of an orbiting, weightless astronaut. Give me an
arrow that says, "This is up" or "This is down."

And so the silent question hangs in the air: Where is
that fixed, enduring rule to which I can defer? No matter
how relativistic and avante-garde I profess to be, my heart
hungers for absolutes. Where is some fact that transcends
culture and circumstance, a word that is older than time?

It seems to me that Norman Maclean raises that question in his *A River Runs through It*. His book and Redford's
movie version of it are about fly fishing and a family's
heartache over a free-spirited son who drinks too much,

lives too fast, and eventually ends his life in a back-alley brawl. But it's more than that: It's about a father's efforts to pass on to his sons the underlying unchanging values of his life. Most of his lessons were taught on trout streams.

Maclean recalls one streamside exchange with his father:

"What have you been reading?" I asked.

"A book," my father replied. It was on the ground on the other side of him. So I would not have to bother to look over his knees to see it, he said, "A good book." Then he told me, "In the part I was reading it says the Word was in the beginning, and that's right. I used to think the water was first, but if you listen carefully you will hear the words are underneath the water."

"That's because you're a preacher first and then a fisherman," I told him. "If you ask Paul, he will tell you that the words were formed out of water."

"No," my father said, "you are not listening carefully. The water runs over the words, Paul will tell you the same thing." I looked to see where the book was left open and knew just enough Greek to recognize *logos* as the Word. I guessed from it and from the argument that I was looking at the first verse of John.

"The river was cut by the world's great flood, and runs over the rocks from the basement of time. . . . Under the rocks are the words."

"In the beginning was the Word," wrote John—a Word that is older than the rocks, a Word that is older than time.

There is an oft-repeated phrase in Elijah's story: "Then the word of the LORD came to Elijah" (1 Kings 17:2, 8; 18:1; 19:9). Behind every utterance of the prophet lay the overwhelming authority of God. When Elijah spoke, he was saying again what God had already said—nothing more, nothing less.

In our relativistic and subjectivist world, the notion of a decisive and final word from God sounds presumptuous. Discovery, dialogue, and debate are more in vogue. You've heard people say it: "Well, that's fine for *you*. But it doesn't have anything to do with *me*."

Yet we must never forget that God's Word is exactly that—*God's* Word. Behind every word we speak lies the infinite power and authority of God himself—an authority mediated through every utterance of ours. Peter wrote, "If anyone speaks, he should do it *as one speaking the very words of God*" (1 Peter 4:11, emphasis added).

In 1 Corinthians 2:6–16 Paul sketches out his theory of knowledge—how we know what we know—and in so doing offers a powerful polemic for the authority of God's Word.

His argument goes like this: God's most profound thoughts were revealed by the Holy Spirit to the prophets and apostles. Those thoughts were translated by the Holy Spirit into actual words on a page—the pages of the original documents on which the prophets and apostles wrote—so that we now have God's profoundest thoughts enshrined forever in that written Word.

Paul concludes by raising the question Isaiah had raised seven centuries before: "Who has known the mind of the Lord?" *We do!* Paul insists; we who wrote the Scriptures have discerned through the Holy Spirit the most profound thoughts of God.

Paul wrote to another church with bold simplicity, "We also thank God continually because, when you received the word of God, which you heard from us, *you accepted it not as the word of men, but as it actually is, the word of God,* which is at work in you who believe (1 Thessalonians 2:13, emphasis added).

We do not run ahead, John wrote (2 John 9), we go back. John was inveighing against certain deceivers for whom everything was flexible and up for grabs. They were progressive in their thinking, always looking for a newer, better word. But, as John insists, we go back—back to the Word "which was from the beginning," back to the prophets and their revelations, back to Jesus and what apostles heard and saw, back to the truth "once for all entrusted to the saints" (Jude 3).

This is our message. We have no other.

The issue of the authority of Scripture is crucial for our thinking about being witnesses for Christ in our skeptical, often hostile world. The question is this: Is God's Word alone sufficient to cut through the lies that cloud unbelievers' minds and debase their lives? Is God's Word alone enough to bring them to repentance and faith?

To that question we can give a resounding *Yes!*

The sufficiency of Scripture is an assumption embedded in Scripture itself and in every biblical admonition to make the truth known.

God's Word is sufficient. God's Word is enough.

**Our task is not to debate the gospel.
Men and women may defy it,
but in their hearts they know it is true.**

Our task is not to debate the gospel, though we must be reasonable in our proclamation of it. Our task is to *announce* it. Men and women may defy it, but in their hearts they know it is true.

Frankly, most people today have never heard an intelligent presentation of the gospel. If you were to ask them what Christians believe, they would answer in terms of certain moral or political stands Christians have taken, but they would have little awareness of the Savior and what he has done for us.

I recall a young man in my Young Life club some years ago who sidled up to me after a club talk and asked me who Jesus was. At first I thought he only wanted me to fill in a few missing details, but as we talked I began to realize he knew *nothing* of the gospel. He was utterly *pagan* in the original sense of that word: He simply had no knowledge of God.

My heart goes out to those like that young man—reared in our post-Christian era with an utter ignorance of the Savior. We must give them something to believe.

The example of Jesus and the apostles is clearly one of instruction. At the beginning of his ministry in Nazareth, Jesus said, "The Spirit of the Lord is on me, because he has anointed me to preach good news to the poor. He has sent me to proclaim freedom for the prisoners and recovery of sight for the blind, to release the oppressed, to proclaim the year of the Lord's favor" (Luke 4:18–19).

After that, Jesus went about all Galilee teaching in the synagogues and proclaiming the gospel of the kingdom. The demands of the crowd never diverted him from that fundamental task. "Everyone is looking for you!" they said after the healings at Capernaum, but Jesus replied, "Let us go somewhere else—to the nearby villages—so I can preach there also. That is why I have come" (Mark 1:37–38).

Jesus commissioned the Twelve and "he sent them out to preach the kingdom of God" (Luke 9:2). When we read the book of Acts, we find them speaking up at every turn, observing the dominant call to preach. Attempts to stop them led them to earnest, united prayer in order that the truth might go out unimpeded, and then they went out to proclaim the gospel. Acts bears witness not only to the power of the Holy Spirit at work in the church, but also to the primary place of proclamation.

When Paul encountered the sophistries and idolatries of Athens, his spirit was deeply "distressed." The word suggests a storm of angry emotions and a militant frame of mind. He was incensed that people could be so thoroughly deceived. Yet what did Paul do? Did he resort to power plays and pressure tactics? Did he invest his time on press releases, demonstrations, protests, product boycotts, or media events?

No.

What did he do? He "reasoned in . . . the marketplace day by day with those who happened to be there" (Acts 17:17).

Paul faced the best and most educated minds of his generation by simply proclaiming the gospel to them. His only hope was that God would shine into every heart and give men and women a glimpse of "the glory of God in the face of Christ" (2 Corinthians 4:6).

Paul wrote, "There will be terrible times in the last days. People will be lovers of themselves, lovers of money, boastful, proud, abusive, disobedient to their parents, ungrateful, unholy, without love, unforgiving, slanderous, without self-control, brutal, not lovers of the good, treacherous, rash, conceited, lovers of pleasure rather than lovers of God" (2 Timothy 3:1–4).

The last days are not some far-off epoch but rather the interadvent period—the period between the first and second comings of Christ (compare Hebrews 1:1). We are living in those days. The response we must make is to "preach the Word . . . in season and out of season . . . with great patience and careful instruction" (2 Timothy 4:2).

"In season and out of season" is Paul's idiom for faithful proclamation. No matter how inclement the climate, no matter how disinclined we are, we must make our Lord known.

"Careful instruction" is another way of saying "intelligent instruction." We must be reasonable in our approach. Our ultimate concern is to reach the emotions and will, but the most direct route is through the mind. This is the hallmark of biblical proclamation.

Read the accounts of Paul's preaching: It is the language of logic and persuasion. The human response is spoken of in terms of "being persuaded" of truth. Luke said, when Paul spoke, "Some of the Jews were persuaded and joined Paul and Silas, as did a large number of God-fearing Greeks and not a few prominent women" (Acts 17:4). Correspondingly, those who responded were said to "believe the truth," "acknowledge the truth," or "obey the truth."

There is great wisdom in frankness. God's truth, spoken boldly, thrusts its sharp point into the soul. "The word of God is living and active. Sharper than any double-edged sword, it penetrates even to dividing soul and spirit, joints and marrow; it judges the thoughts and attitudes of the heart" (Hebrews 4:12). It penetrates into that region of feelings, dispositions, and impressions.

Paul said, "By setting forth the truth plainly we commend ourselves to every man's conscience in the sight of God" (2 Corinthians 4:2).

God's Word requires little or no ornamentation. It simply needs to be stated.

Truth sets up a sympathetic vibration in the soul. God's law is written there, which means that everything we say has been heard before. When we speak truth, the conscience *resonates* with it. The hardest heart is at the mercy of God's Word.

Jesus said, "When he [the Spirit of Truth] comes, he will convict the world of guilt in regard to sin and righteousness and judgment: in regard to sin, because men do not believe in me; in regard to righteousness, because I am going to the Father, where you can see me no longer; and in regard to judgment, because the prince of this world now stands condemned" (John 16:8–11).

Often we read this verse as though the Holy Spirit corroborates our witness. Actually, it's the other way around. Our witness corroborates the witness that the Holy Spirit has already given! He precedes us and prepares every human heart.

The Spirit of God impresses three facts upon the world: The first is the sin of unbelief in God's Son—the *only* sin which God now holds against the world. God does not judge the down-and-out for their drunkenness, drug-pushing, prostitution, or pimping. Nor does he judge the up-and-out for their sullen pride, though it breaks his heart to see the objects of his great love ruining themselves with these devices. *All these vile acts have been paid for.*

The only sin that God reckons against unbelievers is unbelief. This is the only sin that he cannot forgive—the "unpardonable sin" of which Jesus spoke (Matthew 12:31). Blasphemy against the Spirit is rigid resistance to his witness to the Savior, our Lord Jesus.

Furthermore, the Spirit establishes in every conscience the existence of a standard by which we weigh ourselves and find ourselves wanting. No one gave us a rule book when we were born, and yet—somehow—we know the rules, don't we? The very fact that we tend to judge others indicates that we know the difference between right and wrong. When we say, "You should . . . ," or "You ought to . . . ," we tip our hand.

Where do we *get* that notion of "should" and "ought"?

How do we *know* the difference between right and wrong?

We know because God has inscribed his law on our hearts. No one needs to tell us right from wrong, and no one needs to tell us that we have gone very far wrong. We know.

Karl Menninger begins his book *Whatever Became of Sin* with a story of a stern-faced, plainly dressed, self-styled prophet who used to haunt the streets of Chicago's Loop. He stood alone and solemnly lifted his right arm, singling out each person who passed by, intoning, "Guilty!" According to Menninger one of those so accused turned to his friend and said, "How did he know?" We *know*. That's how we know.

And finally, the Spirit of God convinces the world of the uncertainty of a judgment. Without being told, we know that there will be a comeuppance, and when it comes we will not do well at all.

You may remember the satirical television program of some years ago, *That Was the Week That Was*. In one segment, David Frost, who was one of the producers of the program, was seated behind a desk. Behind him were two doors, one labeled Hell, the other, Heaven. A series of men and women approached the desk with only one question: "Which way do I go?"

In each case Frost answered, "You know."

Without a word, each one shuffled off to hell.

The Spirit of God has written the truth indelibly on every soul. Our witness corroborates his witness. When we proclaim God's truth, people *know*.

We must be bold in our proclamation, but we must never bully people. "He who wins by force hath won but half his foe," Emerson said.

Paul wrote that we must fight the *good* fight. It is notable that Paul used the adjective *good* here. The word means "pleasant" or "beautiful." Though we must "contend for the faith," as Jude said (verse 3), we must not be contentious—quarrelsome, argumentative, unpleasant, and in people's faces.

Matthew said of Jesus, quoting an Old Testament forecast, "He will not quarrel or cry out; no one will hear his voice in the streets" (Matthew 12:19). The word translated "quarrel" means "to wrangle" and is used to describe the calm temper of Jesus in contrast with the vehemence of the Jewish scholars wrangling about tenets and practices.

Paul wrote:

The Lord's servant must not quarrel; instead, he must be kind to everyone, able to teach, not resentful. Those who oppose him he must gently instruct, in the hope that God will grant them repentance leading them to a knowledge of the truth, and that they will come to their senses and escape from the trap of the devil, who has taken them captive to do his will. (2 Timothy 2:24–26)

Faith can never be foisted on another. We cannot compel obedience. Railing at people, threats of punishment or harm, subtle manipulation, biting sarcasm, and attempts to coerce are all contrary to the spirit of Christ. Consent must be gained by gentle persuasion and reason. "The act of faith," said W. H. Auden, "still remains an act of choice which no one can force upon another."

Although we may engage in controversy from time to time, woe be unto us if we revel in it. Some of us are always looking for a fight, like the Irishman who stopped to watch a street fight and inquired, "Is this a private fight or can anyone join in?"

Sad to say, the fighting is often dirty—fist shaking, name calling, fierce, angry faces, and verbal abuse. Discussion and debate on the facts is one thing; fury, innuendo, and insult is another. When we resort to bitter abuse, we lose our moral and rational force, and what's worse, we actually *push people away* from the living God who loves and reaches out to them. When we do so, we're sure of just one ally—the Devil.

> **Without kindness, truth is just so much dogma. Without truth, kindness is mere sentimentality.**

We must be humble: courteous in our demeanor, not defensive in our posture, gently instructing those who oppose the truth in the hope that God will grant repentance leading to a knowledge of the truth. How is it that we keep forgetting? Those who oppose the gospel are not the enemy. They are the *victims* of the enemy who have been taken captive by him to do his will. It's sinful to pin them wriggling against the wall—wrong and counterproductive. They will never be won that way.

Manner and message are inextricably linked; one goes with the other. Without kindness, truth is just so much dogma. Without truth, kindness is mere sentimentality. Only God's truth delivered with loving kindness has power to bring about consent.

Peter says we must be prepared to answer those who ask us a reason for the hope we have, but we must "do this with gentleness and respect" (1 Peter 3:15). In our enthusiasm we must not resort to severity. Others' salvation depends on it. The Good News only sounds good when it's delivered with good manners.

Elijah's call was to deliver his blunt message and walk out, leaving his words to resonate in Ahab's heart. There are some situations that call for such stern measures, but most of the time God has a milder way.

The best proclamation takes place in the context of loving relationships. We must learn from our Lord the principle he enunciated and exemplified so well: there is no lasting influence without loving contact. One of the distinctive features of Jesus' ministry was his inclination to eat and drink with irreligious and morally untidy people even though it scandalized the clergy and other religious folk of his day. The immediate and unthinkable conclusion was that he was the friend of sinners, and as it turns out, he is: "The Son of Man came to seek and to save what was lost (Luke 19:10)."

Our Lord spent time with unbelievers—strolling along streams and seashores, sitting around campfires, going to parties, socializing, chatting, being neighborly.

Tertullian, an early Roman Christian, described Christians of his day this way: "We live among you [non-Christians], eat the same food, wear the same clothes, have the same habits and the same necessities of existence. We are not Gymnosophists [a kooky sect encountered in India by Alexander the Great] who dwell in the woods and exile ourselves from ordinary forum, nor market, not bath, nor booth, nor workshop, nor inn. . . . We sail with you, we fight with you, we till the ground with you, we join with you in business ventures."

Friendships with those in the world are forged by being *with* them. The King James Version translators put it this way: "A man that hath friends must shew himself friendly" (Proverbs 18:24). The text doesn't really say that, but I still like that translation. It enshrines a convention: A friend is someone you befriend, or put another way, the way to make a friend is to *be* one. With that perspective in mind, we'll never run out of friends. The whole world is full of them.

But friendship entails more than mere togetherness and small talk. It means sharing in one way or another what we know of our Lord. As he teaches us new things about himself, we must give those thoughts away.

A real friend is one who leaves God's words with another.

> It may be quiet counsel to a confused soul.
> It may be a word of grace to a troubled conscience.
> It may be a word of comfort or a kindly stated correction that inexplicably rings true.
> It may be an off-the-cuff comment that leaves another longing for more.
> It may be a partial or complete explanation of the gospel.

I can't tell you exactly what to say. No book or pamphlet can tell you what to say. There are no directives, instructions, or outlines that always work. Witness must come from the heart, an elaboration of what we ourselves have seen and heard. I can only tell you that as you walk with our Lord and learn from him, he will give you "an instructed tongue, to know the word that sustains the weary" (Isaiah 50:4).

You may be artless and inarticulate in your witness at first, but as a friend of mine says, if a thing is worth doing, it's worth doing poorly. Even an awkwardly spoken word is better than no word at all. And even if no fruit is immediately gathered, in the sense that our friends seem no closer to God, something has happened: A seed has been dropped into the soil and the life in that seed will cause it to grow.

Our Lord promised, "[My word] will not return to me empty, but will accomplish what I desire and achieve the purpose for which I sent it" (Isaiah 55:11).

People's needs are excruciatingly deep. They cry "out of the depths," as the psalmist did (Psalm 130:1). How often we find ourselves in conversations with needy people and feel at an utter loss to know what to say. How can we speak to another's profound necessities? How can we dispel the illusions that permeate society and disillusion it? How can we "speak a word in season to him that is weary"?

Jesus said of those times that we must not worry about what to say or how to say it. "At that time you will be given what to say" (Matthew 10:19). That's not to say that God fills our minds with thoughts we've never had before but rather that he takes from a reservoir of accumulated truth those things that he wants us to say.

"What I tell you in the dark," Jesus said, "speak in the daylight; what is whispered in your ear, proclaim from the roofs" (verse 27). These words are applicable to all. Our Lord speaks to us in solitude. There he tells us eternal and infinite secrets. There our eyes begin to see what only he can see; there our ears begin to detect the subtle undertones of his voice.

The most persuasive words are spoken by those who are taught by God himself. John wrote:

That which was from the beginning, which we have heard, which we have seen with our eyes, which we have looked at and our hands have touched—this we proclaim concerning the Word of life. The life appeared; we have seen it and testify to it, and we proclaim to you the eternal life, which was with the Father and has appeared to us. We proclaim to you what we have seen and heard, so that you also may have fellowship with us. And our fellowship is with the Father and with his Son, Jesus Christ.
(1 John 1:1–3)

Telling people what others have taught us doesn't have much impact on them. It plays with the head but it does not penetrate the heart. The best witness is telling others what we ourselves have heard, what we have seen with our eyes, what we have looked at and our hands have touched.

The essential thing is to sit at Jesus' feet and learn from him.

The more we receive, the more we have to give.

It's through prayerful, thoughtful Bible study and quiet meditation that he speaks from his depths to ours. We must stay in his presence until he entrusts us with his word.

I create "praise on the lips," God says (Isaiah 57:19). Our words are like fruit: the final reason for a tree's existence. It's

why we are being cultivated. Good words come from within, the final product of God's Word hidden away in our
hearts.

The servant of the Lord said:

The Sovereign LORD has given me an instructed tongue,
    to know the word that sustains the weary.
He wakens me morning by morning,
    wakens my ear to listen like one being taught.

—Isaiah 50:4

We should begin each day with a desire to "listen like
one being taught." We should read the Word from start to
finish, over and over again, reflecting on what God is saying to us. We should give ourselves time for prayerful contemplation until God's heart is revealed and our hearts are
exposed.

We should think of God as present and speaking to us,
disclosing his mind and emotions and will. We should
meditate on his words until his mind begins to inform
ours—till we know what he knows, feel what he feels, want
what he wants, enjoy what he enjoys, desire what he
desires, love what he loves, hate what he hates. Of the reading and writing of books there is no end—even of books
about God. The main thing is to give ourselves to the words
that are "given by one Shepherd" (Ecclesiastes 12:11) and
then to give those words away.

There is a natural law: That which is not given away
soon passes away. If we do not give God's words to others
we will not have them much longer. They will fade away.
Jesus said, "Whoever has will be given more, and he will
have an abundance. Whoever does not have, even what he

has will be taken from him" (Matthew 13:12). The more we give, the more we have to give away.

God's profound and most powerful thoughts are revealed to those who want them and who share them with others.

God's profound and most powerful thoughts are revealed to those who want them and who share them with others. If you love truth and long for it, he will disclose his heart and mind to you.

You will then have something to say.

Albert Einstein was once the featured speaker at a dinner given at Swarthmore College. When it was time for him to speak, he astonished everyone when he stood up and said, "I have nothing to say," and sat down. A few seconds later he stood up and said, "In case I have something to say, I will come back and say it." Six months later he wired the president of the college and said, "Now I have something to say." Another dinner was held and he gave his speech.

If you have nothing to say, please cure your ignorance. Sit at Jesus' feet. Listen and learn from him.

If you have nothing to say, please cure your ignorance. Sit at Jesus' feet. Listen and learn from him. As one of MacDonald's characters put it, "Hide yersel' in God, and when ye rise before men, speak oot o' that secret place—

and fear naethin! Look your people straight in the eye and say what at the moment ye think and feel, and dinna hesitate to give them the best ye hae."

God's word, spoken with quiet assurance, moves heaven and earth. When we draw that sword we join the angelic hosts by which the world, the flesh, and the Devil are overthrown.

God's Word, spoken with quiet assurance, moves heaven and earth. When we draw that sword, we join the angelic hosts by which the world, the flesh, and the Devil are overthrown.

Seeing Deeper

1. When Elijah first spoke to Ahab in 1 Kings 17, what was his message? Do you hold onto that message as you face each day?

2. The author states, "Behind the fakery [of Baalism] was a monstrous reality." Behind evil there is EVIL. How are those who serve evil rewarded today? Why, then, does the attraction continue?

3. In Psalm 11:3, David wrote: "When the foundations are being destroyed, what can the righteous do?" Elijah lived in an era when God's Word and God's righteous

standards for the nation had been summarily rejected.
The godly in the land were so few and so lacking in
influence and the restraint of evil that Elijah concluded
he was the only one left zealous of God.

How would you compare our nation's rejection of
the Bible and Christianity with Israel's rejection of
Yahweh? We, too, live in a land where many have not
bent the knee to Baal, but how has the rejection and
undermining of God's Word in our culture affected even
believers?

4. Read Romans 1:18–20 and Hebrews 4:12. Sometimes we
find ourselves reluctant in our witness for Christ, concerned about our powers of persuasion or our abilities
to carry the debate. But what did the author say would
enlighten the unbeliever? Why?

5. The author said two things were needed to rescue victims deceived by the Evil One—truth and attitude. How
can we most effectively give them the truth? What does
attitude have to do with the truth? (See Acts 17:4 and
2 Timothy 2:23–26.)

6. What's more persuasive than an "explanation" of God?
Why?

7. If you fear that you have nothing to say, what does the
author encourage you to do?

Though we may seem to be doing nothing worthwhile in this world, we can be doing everything worthwhile if our lives are being styled by God's grace. Set aside through sickness or seclusion, we can still be immensely prolific. Though we may be bedridden or housebound, our holiness by itself can yet bear fruit. To be useful, we don't have to be good for anything—just good. Good people do more good than they ever know. Lighthouse keepers never know how many ships they have turned away from the rocks. Their duty is to shine, not to look for results.

Chapter Five

Down by the Riverside

He hath a daily beauty in his life that makes me ugly.
—Shakespeare

Then the word of the LORD came to Elijah: "Leave here, turn east-
ward and hide in the ravine of Kerith, east of the Jordan. You will
drink from the brook, and I have ordered the ravens to feed you
there." So he did what the LORD had told him. He went to the Kerith
Ravine, east of the Jordan, and stayed there. (1 Kings 17:2–5)

Elijah was told to hide himself in a desolate ravine.

The word of the Lord directed him to Kerith, one of many deep wadis that wind their way through the wilderness east of the Jordan River. In this stark and dreary place he found himself utterly alone.

But alone with God.

The wilderness was the place of preparation for the work God had called him to do.

The wilderness may be the best place in the world to get to know God. Israel spent time there. So did Moses, David, Jesus, and Paul. "Remote from man, with God they passed their days."

The wilderness is the place of soul-making, to use that quaint old Quaker phrase. Soul-making is essential. We do not make our mark on the world by instinct, intellect, education, personality, humor, appearance, or charm. Influence comes from *within*. It is a matter of the heart. It cannot be quantified or codified—put into a two-step or ten-step process. It can't be gained at a weekend seminar or obtained from a correspondence course. It is the result of the work God is doing in our souls.

And that work is always done in secret.

In our very own "Kerith."

Hide yourself, God said to Elijah. Kerith represents the hidden life no one sees but God. Jesus said, "Go into your room, close the door and pray to your Father, who is unseen. Then your Father, who sees what is done in secret, will reward you" (Matthew 6:6).

Call it what you may—quiet time, solitude, retreat—it is a time and place in which we meet our Lord in adoration and worship. Worship is the key to everything—the only thing that is absolutely necessary.

Henri Nouwen once asked Mother Teresa how he could make his ministry more convincing. She answered with characteristic simplicity: "Spend one hour a day in devotion to Jesus, Henri, and you'll be all right."

I think of Mary and Martha, whose home Jesus often entered. He always found it perfectly suited to his needs. He began to teach, and Mary—who instinctively knew the most crucial, pressing need of the day—sat at his feet, absorbing his presence and everything he had to say.

Martha, who had much to do for Jesus, busied herself with work and became "distracted by all the preparations that had to be made," hustling about the place to make it more presentable, doing things for Jesus that he didn't want done at all.

Jesus said in his kindly way that what Martha was doing was much ado about nothing. "Martha, Martha," he said, "you are worried and upset about many things, but only one thing is needed. Mary has chosen what is better, and it will not be taken away from her" (Luke 10:41–42). Mary was worshiping Jesus. Martha was trying to do the work of God.

Whether in a comfortable living room or the bottom of a dry ravine, there is no substitute for time spent at the feet of the Lord.

Jesus in the Wilderness

Jesus often went into the wilderness.

When evening came, he was there alone. (Matthew 14:23)

It was not mere time alone he craved—as much as his humanity may have longed for solitude. He was there alone *with God*. On especially difficult days, he "went out to a mountainside to pray, and spent the night praying to God" (Luke 6:12). It was his practice, his tradition, his delight. Thirty-something years old might seem astonishingly young to those of us crowding sixty or seventy, yet it was time enough for the Carpenter of Nazareth to have established unshakable life habits.

> He knew what to do when life closed in.
> He knew where to go when demands piled high.
> He knew whom to seek when pressures multiplied.

The days and nights Jesus spent in isolation repaired the damage done by the crowds. There he walked among the trees, basked in his Father's affection and love, and listened to his counsel. These times of solitude drew our Lord away from what *seemed* to be true and renewed his faith in "things not seen." Each time, he returned from the wilderness with vision restored, ready to tell others what he had seen and heard: "I am telling you what I have seen in the Father's presence," he would say (John 8:38).

Jesus constantly impressed upon his disciples the necessity of time alone with God: "Because so many people were coming and going that they did not even have a chance to eat, he said to them, 'Come with me by yourselves to a quiet place and get some rest' " (Mark 6:31).

We too must find that place of revelation and rest. God will give us a fresh vision of himself each day if we will take time to be with him, if we will approach him with a quiet and expectant heart.

A. W. Tozer wrote, "Retire from the world each day to some private spot. . . . Stay in the secret place till the surrounding noises begin to fade out of your heart and a sense of God's presence envelops you."

The vision takes time.

There is no easy path.

True life change is the result of extended periods spent sitting at our Lord's feet, listening to his words, and seeking his face. "Look to the LORD and his strength; seek his face always," Israel's poet said (Psalm 105:4). We cannot convince ourselves of his presence; we cannot make our hearts believe and make our eyes see. *He* must make his reinforcing presence real. "If you seek him, he will be found by you" (1 Chronicles 28:9).

Something very significant happens through these established times of worship: we begin to gain a heart-connection with God.

> We come to love what he loves.
> We come to hate what he hates.
> We come to think what he thinks.
> We come to see what he sees.
> We begin to concern ourselves with
>   his concerns.

This is "the place where (our Lord) remodels us in his image," wrote Nouwen. Without this solitude, we have nothing to say to others—and no energy to say it. Without it we live trivial lives with no influence on others.

"Moses used to take a tent and pitch it outside the camp some distance away, calling it the 'tent of meeting' " (Exodus 33:7), from which he came out to meet with his people. We need our own sanctuary to which we can retire for worship—our special place of meeting—from which we can emerge to bring help to others.

The more we receive, the more we have to give. Solitude gives us a new sense of the reality of God's presence and a new way of looking at everything. The main thing is not what we say but what God has said to us and what he then says to others.

"There is a chamber," MacDonald wrote, "a chamber in God himself which none can enter but the one, the individual, the particular man. Out of which chamber that man has to bring revelation and strength for his brethren. This is that for which he was made—to reveal the secret things of the Father."

Paul said to Timothy, "Watch your life and doctrine closely. Persevere in them, because if you do, you will save both yourself and your hearers" (1 Timothy 4:16). It's vital to stay in touch with our Lord. We cannot draw others to know him unless we ourselves are drawing near to God. Saving ourselves is the first step toward saving others.

We need solitude, not mere privacy and time alone, but time alone with God, a specific time and place to read his Word, to pray, to worship, a beginning place from which we can work God's work in the world.

Several years ago Dick Hillis, that rugged old China warrior and founder of Overseas Crusades, wrote this to me: "The main thing is to love the Lord our God with all our heart [our center of affection and love], our soul [the center of our daily living], our mind [the center of all our thinking], our strength [the center of all our wealth and possessions]. I think if we practice that love a little more, we will be better servants, better under-shepherds than we have ever been."

Influence grows out of worship. Without that preoccupation, we have nothing to give a cynical, desperately unhappy, and unsettled world.

In 1966, during the closing service of the World Congress on Evangelism in the Kongresshalle in Berlin, Germany, Billy Graham spoke of the need for "a gentleness and a kindness and a love and a forgiveness and a compassion" that will mark us as different from the world. "We must be a holy people," he said.

As an illustration of the power of personal holiness, he spoke of the conversion of Dr. H. C. Morrison, founder of Asbury Theological Seminary. He described a day many years ago when Morrison, as a farm worker, was plowing in a field. Looking down the road, he saw an old Methodist circuit rider coming by on his horse.

Morrison had seen the elderly gentleman before and knew him to be a gracious, godly man. As he watched the old saint go by, Morrison felt the power of God's presence, and a great sense of conviction of sin came over him. He dropped to his knees. And there, between the furrows in his field, alone, he gave his life to God.

When he concluded the story, Billy Graham earnestly prayed, "Oh, God, make me a holy man—a holy man."

It all begins in the silence of the wilderness. Alone with God.

A Declaration of Dependence

The record in 1 Kings 17 goes on to say:

> *The ravens brought him bread and meat in the morning and bread and meat in the evening, and he drank from the brook.* (verse 6)

It's contrary to nature to suppose that a wadi like Kerith would continue to flow in the midst of drought, or that ravens, from which we get our word *ravenous* would give their food to a human.

More contrary still that ravens would bring it morning and evening exactly on time. In years to come, Elijah must have looked back to the brook with a great deal of satisfaction. There he learned that God works through weak and obscure instruments to do his work for him.

How often we look to the rich and famous to get the job done. Dr. Martyn Lloyd-Jones once said:

> We Christians often quote "not by might nor by power, but by my spirit saith the Lord," and yet in practice we seem to rely upon the mighty dollar and the power of the press and

advertising. We seem to think that our influence will depend on our technique and the program we can put forward and that it would be the numbers, the largeness, the bigness that would prove effective. We seem to have forgotten that God has done most of his deeds in the church throughout its history through remnants. We seem to have forgotten the great story of Gideon, for instance, and how God insisted on reducing the 32,000 men down to 300 before he would make use of them. We have become fascinated by the idea of bigness, and we are quite convinced that if we can only stage, yes, that's the word, stage something really big before the world, we will shake it and produce a mighty religious awakening. That seems to be the modern conception of authority.

But as Jesus said, "What is highly valued among men is detestable in God's sight" (Luke 16:15). God does not look for powerful instruments but for instruments that can be wielded by his power.

Kerith represents our lifelong task of learning *dependence*. It is the place where we learn that all things are done by faith. Without faith it is impossible to please God, and without it nothing enduring gets done.

The Pharisees once asked Jesus what they could do to work for God. Jesus replied: "The work of God is this: to *believe* in the one he has sent" (John 6:28–29, emphasis added). How inconceivable to think that God would be so hard up that he must rely on human beings to get his work done! How audacious of us to think we must do it. Only God can bring salvation to the world. Our work is not to work but to believe in the work he has finished and to enter his rest. That's true of our own salvation as well as the salvation of others.

What we do is never enough. There are rival powers that are strong enough to make our best laid plans go awry. "Old Adam is too strong for young Philip," Luther's sidekick, Philip Melanchthon, lamented. If we are to do anything at all for ourselves or for others, it must be done by faith. "Without me," Jesus reminded his men, "you can do nothing."

Still, it's no easy task to persuade folks like you and me to stop working. We'll do almost anything but rest. In this world, value comes from *what we do,* and of course, there is always more to do. Life for us is one prolonged and dedicated struggle to fix everything that's broken and achieve perfection in all we do.

Unfortunately, our work habits carry over to our relationship with our Lord and to our work for him. We're driven and compulsive in our obedience—always hustling and hoping to do more. Eventually, of course, we get weary and worn down and want to give up.

Yet Jesus said his yoke is *easy.* Could it be?

Jesus promised *rest.* Is that possible?

Spiritual maturity is not measured by the amount of work we accomplish.

Why, then, are so many of God's faithful workers sustaining stress fractures? Why are so many choice servants of Christ coming unraveled, unhinged, and undone? Why do so many of us feel dried up, emptied out, and overwhelmed by the tasks before us? Could there be something wrong with the way we are going about our labor for the Lord? Could it be that we're not wearing Jesus' yoke?

"Busy Christian," John White said, ought to sound like "adulterous wife" to us. The two ideas are shockingly incongruent. Busyness is not a Christian virtue and spiritual maturity is not measured by the amount of work we accomplish—no matter what we're busy doing or how much we get done.

When you think about it, out Lord was never that busy. Yes, he had an infinite job to do and only three and a half years to do it, yet there was very little effort in his work. His pace was always measured and slow. The only person he ever told to get busy was Judas: "What you have to do, do more quickly," he said.

Activity is no good apart from God. His work is done "not by might nor by power, but by [his] Spirit" (Zechariah 4:6). As the screen-saver text I put on my Macintosh keeps reminding me: *"He* will do it" (1 Thessalonians 5:24, emphasis added). That's not only a screen-saver—it's a life-saver!

From the very beginning, God has been concerned about our compulsive work habits, trying to get us to stop working so hard and rest. That's why he instituted the sign of the Sabbath: "Remember the Sabbath day," he said, "by keeping it holy [special]. Six days you shall labor and do all your work, but the seventh day is a Sabbath to the LORD your God. *On it you shall not do any work*" (Exodus 20:8–10, emphasis added).

The Sabbath wasn't made for the worshiping saint. Worship went on every day in Israel. It was given because God has already done all the work that needs to be done and is now himself resting: "For in six days the LORD made the heavens and the earth, the sea, and all that is in them, but he rested on the seventh day. *Therefore* the LORD blessed the Sabbath day and made it holy" (verse 11, emphasis added).

God worked very hard for six days and then stopped his labor to relax and luxuriate in what he had done: "God saw all that he had made, and it was very good" (Genesis 1:31).

My, he mused, isn't it *beautiful?*

The Israelite who observed God's Sabbath was doing what God was doing—he was resting because God had done all his work for him. There wasn't anything left to do.

Israel's Sabbath was essentially a test of faith in God's provision. To make that point specific he said in another place, "You shall work six days, but on the seventh you shall rest; even during plowing time and harvest you shall rest" (Exodus 34:21 NASB). In the busiest times of the year, when hard workers thought they ought to work harder, God wouldn't let them work every day. They had to rest and rely on *God's* activity. By so doing they learned that even when they weren't working, things were getting done.

It's hard to rest when there's so much to be done, but God wanted his people to know that resting is one of the most important things human beings can do. To make his point, he had to make Sabbath-breaking a capital offense before anyone got the message (see Numbers 15:32–36).

God also taught Israel about Sabbath-keeping through the conquest and settlement of Canaan. He promised to drive out the Canaanites and to give Israel rest in that place. He promised to fight their enemies for them. In essence, they were fighting battles that were *already won.* But over the long haul, the good news they heard didn't benefit them because they really didn't believe it. And so, God swore, "They shall never enter my rest." And they didn't.

The author of Hebrews argues that we too must learn to rest, while "the promise of entering his rest still stands" (4:1). Our lives depend on it. We should "be careful" lest we get left behind like those whose carcasses littered the Sinai. It's a serious matter to work and get no rest. We may work ourselves to death.

We, like Israel, have heard the good news that God is for us and has been working for us from the beginning— bringing us home to him, doing his work of changing us, directing our lives, doing whatever has to be done. Whatever we do, whether it is giving up all we have to follow Jesus, putting down malice, injustice, anger, wrong, and selfishness in our own souls, or proclaiming the good news to others, it is done by entering his rest. Our salvation, our sanctification, our service is accomplished by believing in what he has already done.

What kept Israel from entering into rest? Underlying all their compulsive self-effort was rank unbelief. Bottom line, they didn't think God had done enough. That's why they complained when they had no food or water; that's why you and I are inclined to rely on our own efforts to make our way into God's favor.

Let's be honest about it: So often we think that everything depends upon us. We figure if anything is to get done, we've got to roll up our sleeves, pitch in, and do it. And so we labor on, working seven days a week, twenty-four hours a day, wearing ourselves out, wearying ourselves— and missing out on all our God intends for us.

The Lord focused his anger on the Pharisees, who burdened his people with such effort-ridden activity. He was never angry with those they burdened. He called them to come to him for rest. But it made him *very* angry when the clergy taught people that God's work must be done by self-effort. That's what made people so weary and destroyed their will to go on. And it's what makes the way for us so long, too. Solomon wrote,

> Unless the LORD builds the house,
>   its builders labor in vain.
> Unless the LORD watches over the city,
>   the watchmen stand guard in vain.
> In vain you rise early
>   and stay up late,
> toiling for food to eat—
>   for he grants sleep to those he loves.
>   —Psalm 127:1–2

Each demand upon us is in reality a demand upon *him*.

We must transfer the burden of responsibility to him and then *leave* it there: "Cast all your anxiety on him because he cares for you" (1 Peter 5:7). Each demand upon us is in reality a demand upon *him*. Our weakness is his opportunity. The disciples' lack of bread did not disconcert our Lord: "He knew what he would do." He always does.

When we fix our eyes on God, we are less inclined to see our own frailty and to feel sorry for ourselves. We see our inability not as an impediment but as the very means by which we untie the hands of the Almighty. Then we hear him say, as he said to Moses, "Now you will see what I will do to Pharaoh: Because of my mighty hand he will let them go" (Exodus 6:1).

Relying on God has to begin every day before anything else is done. If you have trouble believing, ask God to help you. Growing faith, like every other virtue, is a job for God! You must ask him to increase your measure of faith, praying, as Mother Teresa prayed, "Lord, give me faith that your work may be done."

When the Brook Runs Dry

Some time later the brook dried up because there had been no rain in the land. (1 Kings 17:7)

For weeks the Kidron brook ran clear, but then as the drought continued, the stream began to dwindle away. Finally there was nothing left but rocks and sand. The pools dried up. Mud congealed and hardened. The birds and animals withdrew.

Elijah was left alone with desolation. But this, too, was part of his preparation.

Suffering is an indispensable part of the process. "God cannot use us deeply until we have suffered greatly," Tozer used to say. God uses best those who have felt the full weight of disaster.

Just before that old soul J. Oswald Sanders went home to be with the Lord, he reminisced with Carolyn and me about an event that occurred early in his ministry. He had just delivered what he considered to be a masterful, compelling message and was leaving the building where he had spoken when he overheard a conversation between two elderly women.

"What did you think of Mr. Sanders's message?" one asked.

"Oh, he'll be alright," the other replied, "when he's suffered awhile."

God's ways are definite and drastic. Saint John of the Cross wrote:

> God perceives the imperfections within us, and because of his love for us, urges us to grow up. His love is not content to leave us in our weakness, and for this reason he takes us into a dark night. He weans us from all of the pleasures by giving us dry times and inward darkness. In doing so he is able to take away all these vices and create virtues within us. Through the dark night pride becomes humility, greed becomes simplicity, wrath becomes contentment, luxury becomes peace, gluttony becomes moderation, envy becomes joy, and sloth becomes strength. No soul will ever grow deep in the spiritual life unless God works passively in that soul by means of the Dark Night.

Kerith is the day of weakness and shame. It is being disregarded, misunderstood, criticized, and accused. It is living with hurtful gestures and critical words. It is losing out as others take our places.

Kerith is the death of our dreams—for ourselves, our marriages, our children. It's waiting in lonely isolation with hope deferred, without promised togetherness, companionship, liberation, and with no end of waiting in sight.

Kerith is obscurity. It is dreary duty that no one sees or applauds. It is humdrum, tedious tasks, some boring, some distasteful, some downright disgusting. It's being unknown, uncelebrated, unnoticed, and unimportant. Kerith delivers us from the need for "men's empty praise"; it makes us satisfied with God's "well done" alone.

Kerith is discovering, to our shame, how little we understand, how much we do not know. It is the sure cure for unholy certainty and woodenheaded dogmatism. It teaches us to be "agnostic," in the sense that we come to the end of ourselves at the end of the day and say, "I'll be honest with you, friend. I just don't know."

We learn that we cannot explain everything that comes our way. It teaches us that sometimes—the only answer is God himself.

Kerith is temptation. "The word in the desert is most attacked by the voices of temptation," T. S. Eliot said. Temptations are sure to come: God permits Satan to sift us like wheat. Temptations humble us, purify us, and teach us to pray.

Kerith is disappointment and debilitating discouragement. It is regret and struggle and failing. It is useless years. It is the agony of spent vice and self-indulgence. It is abject failure through which we learn that our wills are incapable of keeping us from sin.

Kerith is humiliation—when we put our worst foot forward and fall flat on our faces. It is how the Lord deals with our presumption and pride. Pride is a vexation to others, but mostly it vexes us. Nothing pleases us if the whole world exists to meet our needs; no one will ever come through. We're always exasperated, offended, disquieted, and tormented. "The only wisdom we can hope to acquire is the wisdom of humility," Eliot said. "Humility is endless."

Kerith is learning to do without—without love, beauty, money, marriage, or health. It is being stripped of friends, father, mother, brother, money, reputation, and even our earnestness for God. It makes us content with God and what he gives—to want but little. It is being weaned away from all other passions but a passion for God.

Kerith is going without feelings, even having no interest in God. It is deliverance from sensuality—our tendency to make feelings the ultimate test of reality. It is growing beyond chance and circumstance. It is learning persistence—not mere resignation but a hardy obedience to a course we know to be right regardless of how we feel.

Kerith makes us thirsty for God. Slowly, steadily, God strips us of all our longings, leaving us with nothing but desire for him alone. We say with Israel's poet:

> *Whom have I in heaven but you?*
> *And earth has nothing I desire besides you.*
> —Psalm 73:25

Suffering can push us away from God or it can draw us close to his heart. It all depends on perspective. If we understand that every event is screened through God's love and chosen for our good, we can accept it with patience, draw near to him, and wait for its outcome. "He who has the 'why' to living can bear with almost any 'how,' " Victor Frankl said.

When we know why—when we see what God is doing with us—and draw near to him, his presence begins to rub off on us: We become more loving, tolerant, joyful, dependable, more stable and strong. We're less likely to waver in the face of opposition or falter because of blame. We're rendered more independent of places or moods; we carry about us a subtle ambiance—a dignity unruffled by insult, untouched by shame. We begin to let go of what we want. We become more mellow, easier to live with, easier to work with, easier to be around.

Adversity enables us to know the human heart. We *understand*. "We can comfort those in any trouble with the comfort we ourselves have received from God" (2 Corinthians 1:4). Suffering shapes us and makes us into instruments that God can use.

The world, obviously, sees no value in suffering. It will always take the easiest and less costly route. But we must see it otherwise. Suffering is God's gift to us, making us more like him than we ever thought possible. "He is the LORD," we say. "Let him do what is good in his eyes" (1 Samuel 3:18).

Our best choice is to be still and submit to God's discipline. We are never so safe as when we yield our wills.

In his love, God tempers each trouble with his gentle mercy. He will not permit us to be stressed beyond endurance: "God is faithful; he will not let you be tempted beyond what you can bear" (1 Corinthians 10:13). That's not to say we will never be stretched beyond what *we* think we can bear! Our Father knows precisely what we can tolerate and selects each adversity with careful scrutiny. He limits its intensity and duration to that which we can endure. He loves us too much to ruin us.

In the meantime, our most difficult days can be full of sweet fellowship and communion with him! In tumults, troubles, and disasters, we abide under the shadow of the Almighty. He is with us; he will keep us in perfect peace.

Goodness: The Real Thing

Kerith makes us useful. There God draws us close to his heart; he teaches us the depths of his wisdom and grace; he allows the sufferings that mature us and make us more like him. Then our lives reflect his holiness and our words reflect his heart and we begin to have a profound effect upon others.

Unbelievers instinctively know the difference between authentic holiness and its counterfeit, self-generated righteousness. Mammy Yokum said that "goodness is better than badness because it's nicer," but I must say that some goodness isn't nice at all. It lacks that cordial love that springs from actual contact with God and is much less interesting to unbelievers than vice.

On the other hand, the goodness that God generates is wonderfully winsome and appealing. As we draw near to him day by day, talking to him, listening to his words, walking with him through our suffering and pain, asking for his help, submitting to his disciplines, his character begins to rub off on us.

Quietly and unobtrusively, his influence softens our wills, makes us thirsty for righteousness, inclines us to do his pleasure, restrains our passions, protects us from evil, makes us ashamed of sinful indulgences, and gives us the courage to choose what is good. In his quiet love, he takes all that's unworthy in us and gradually turns it into good.

Holiness is a gift of God. "There is no true virtue without a miracle," Augustine said. God must work his magic on us. Then we speak from great depth and with profound authority, and there is no authority quite so compelling.

Those whom God is making good have an extraordinary effect on others. They leave behind "strangely warmed" hearts. Others take note that we have been with Jesus. We leave behind his fragrance—an unforgettable ambiance, a sweet aroma (2 Corinthians 2:14–15). The memory lingers and leaves others longing for more.

Some years ago Carolyn and I attended a community concert in Boise that featured an alto soloist. What a voice! She awed us with her rich voice and astonishing range. On the way out, a young woman who had accompanied us, herself a musician, said to Carolyn, "I wish I could take lessons from her." Would that we so lived that others would want to take lessons from us.

Fictionalized evil always looks good, while fictionalized good always looks boring and dull. In reality, the opposite is true. *Real* evil plunges people into boredom and despair while *real* goodness is wonderfully appealing. Unbelievers are attracted when they see it in others—and they want to know more.

The tragedy of having no contact with God is that we are rendered shallow and superficial. We're easily dismissed, easily forgotten. Conversely, the presence of a woman or a man who is being crafted by God is as powerful as God himself and, to some small extent, just as awesome.

And what will that power look like?

It usually doesn't look like anything at all.

When we *try* to be influential we become too aggressive and intrusive.

Spiritual power is rarely apparent. It is not a function of charm and chutzpah, nor is it a matter of vast knowledge, strength of will, or personal magnetism. Self-conscious and self-effected influence is always pretentious. When we *try* to be influential, we become too aggressive and intrusive. Our actions seem forced and our words ring hollow. True authority is a subtle redolence, an unaffected persuasion that pervades people's thoughts and gently goads them toward God.

The Lord said of his Servant:

> *Here is my servant, whom I uphold,*
> > *my chosen one in whom I delight;*
> *I will put my Spirit on him*
> > *and he will bring justice to the nations.*
> *He will not shout or cry out,*
> > *or raise his voice in the streets.*
> *A bruised reed he will not break,*
> > *and a smoldering wick he will not snuff out.*
> *In faithfulness he will bring forth justice;*
> > *he will not falter or be discouraged*
> *till he establishes justice on earth.*
> > *In his law the islands will put their hope.*
>
> —Isaiah 42:1–4

Here is one who brought salvation to the world. And how did he do it? Not by strength of personality or will but by the gentle persuasion of a Spirit-filled, godlike life.

Peter urges: "Make every effort to add to your faith goodness; and to goodness, knowledge; and to knowledge, self-control; and to self-control, perseverance; and to perseverance, godliness; and to godliness, brotherly kindness; and to brotherly kindness, love. For if you possess these qualities in increasing measure, they will keep you from being ineffective and unproductive" (2 Peter 1:5–8).

Effectiveness and productivity stem from what we are. Though we may seem to be doing nothing worthwhile in this world, we can be doing everything worthwhile if our lives are being styled by God's grace. Set aside through sickness or seclusion, we can still be immensely prolific. Though we may be bedridden or housebound, our holiness by itself can yet bear fruit. To be useful, we don't have to be good for anything—just good.

Good people do more good than they ever know. Lighthouse keepers never know how many ships they have turned away from the rocks. Their duty is to shine not to look for results. We must be content to do the will of God where we are. We may not see the results that our characters have wrought, but God sees and we can be certain that "he will not forget [our] work" (Hebrews 6:10).

"Dear friends . . . ," Peter wrote, "Live such good lives among the pagans that . . . they may see your good deeds and glorify God on the day he visits us" (1 Peter 2:11–12). May we so live that men and women will be drawn to love our Lord and welcome him on the day he comes to make his inspection of every heart.

> *Just allow people to see Jesus in you*
> *to see how you pray*
> *to see how you lead a pure life*
> *to see how you deal with your family*
> *to see how much peace there is in your family*
> *Then you can look straight into their eyes and say*
> *"This is the way."*
> *You speak from life, you speak from experience.*
> —Mother Teresa

"Well, that's fine for Mother Teresa," you may say, "but I'm me, and I'm not there yet! I have too much growing to do."

No matter. It is not perfection that impresses others and makes them hunger for God but purity of intention. It is "willing one will," as Kierkegaard said—wanting with all of our hearts what God wants and waiting for him to bring it about.

We're under construction. God isn't finished with us yet. "This life is not godliness," Luther said, "but the process of becoming godly, not health but the process of becoming healthy, not being but becoming, not rest but exercise. The process is not yet finished, but it is actually going on. This is not the goal, but it is the right road. At present everything does not gleam and sparkle, but everything is being cleansed."

God's processes are adequate to deal with sin. We must be comfortable with ourselves in process. God heals by degrees. We grow slowly but steadily from one degree of likeness to the next—inch by inch, here a little, there a little. "We, who with unveiled faces all reflect the Lord's glory, are being transformed into his likeness with ever-increasing glory, which comes from the Lord, who is the Spirit" (2 Corinthians 3:18).

Gain is gain, however small.

A friend of mine tells about a morning when she was smarting from an angry argument with her husband. Ranting around the kitchen, slamming cabinet doors, and swearing under her breath, she glanced out of her screen door and into the startled eyes of a non-Christian neighbor to whom she had been witnessing for some time.

My friend's anger turned into embarrassed laughter. She asked her friend in, explained her fury, and asked her forgiveness. Then she said with complete candor, "Susan, God isn't through with me yet."

God doesn't waste anything—even our sin.

"Even from our sin," Augustine said, "God can draw good." He discerns the possibilities in the most humiliating and damaging situations and utilizes them for his intended purpose. God doesn't waste anything—even our sin.

Salt and Light

Jesus said to a group of obscure, uncelebrated people, "You [and you alone] are the salt of the earth. . . . You [and you alone] are the light of the world. . . . Let your light shine before men, that they may see your good deeds and praise your Father in heaven" (Matthew 5:13–16).

Jesus' assertion that this set of insignificant people was the salt of the earth must have sounded absurd to those who heard him, particularly in view of the entrenched pride and sophistication of the Roman Empire. These were ordinary people, far from the centers of power and prestige. Few had much education. None had any political clout. Most of them had never been more than twenty miles from home.

Yet Jesus affirmed that

they could arrest the spread of corruption in their home towns

they could dispel the illusions that clouded their neighbors' minds

they were the catalysts who could cleanse society and correct the lies that debased it.

they were like lanterns held high, spilling

warm, welcoming light on a cold, murky twilight.

And so it is today. The real business of God is done by those whose lives are characterized by godliness. These folks, even in small numbers, are the salt of the earth and the radiant light of a world at dusk.

Peter asks on the eve of destruction, "What kind of people ought you to *be?* You ought to live holy and godly lives" (2 Peter 3:11, emphasis added).

Sometimes, the whole process begins in the bottom of a dry ravine.

Don't despise it, my friend.

Seeing Deeper

1. Read 1 Samuel 3:18, Psalm 73:25, and 1 Peter 5:7. God didn't hide Elijah in a city among the masses nor send him to a safe haven such as Egypt or Antioch. Instead, he placed him in a lonely, desolate ravine. Why? What is your typical response when you find yourself in desolate circumstances?

2. The author relates the story of a circuit rider whose holy life had such an impact on H. C. Morrison that the young man fell to his knees and gave his life to God after the preacher simply rode by the field where he was working! Where are the holy people today? Do you know holy people whose lives are so marked by the presence of Christ that they impact people wherever they go?

3. Read again the familiar story of Luke 10:38–42. We know well what the two sisters were doing: Martha was _____ and Mary was _____ . What was Martha forfeiting—and for what gain? Describe periods in your life when you made the Martha choice—and when the Mary choice. Which choice most characterizes your life right now?

4. Read Matthew 11:28. "If being God's worker is wearing us out these days," says the author, "then there's something wrong with the way we're going about it." Why do we insist on working harder and faster?

5. Without a fresh vision of God, we're told "we have nothing to say." In the absence of such a vision, "we live trivial lives with no influence on others . . . and we are rendered shallow and superficial." Honestly and realistically—what would it take in your life to acquire or renew such a life-changing vision of your God?

6. The author writes: "Good people do more good than they ever know. Lighthouse keepers never know how many ships have turned away from the rocks. Their duty is to shine not to look for results." Read Matthew 5:14–16 and 1 Peter 2:11–12. As honestly as you can, evaluate the shine factor in your own life. Has God so rubbed off on you, as a result of your time with him, that you reflect him to others?

7. What has impacted you most from this
chapter?

...cial Plastic Surgery/Sinus Surgery

E. BRADLEY STRONG, M.D.
Assistant Professor, Otolaryngology
Co-Director Image Guided Surgery Program

Area Code 916
734-5400 Appointments
734-3109 Advice Nurse
451-8124 Referral Fax
734-2011 Emergency

Department of Otolaryngology
...a Blvd. Suite 7200

God's will is easy to find—if we want it. Really, the only people who miss his will are those who have no use for it. The months and years may show we've taken a strange, roundabout way, but if our hearts are right, our feet will never go astray. We will know what God wants us to do. I cannot tell you how you will know, but I can tell you that when you have to know (and not necessarily before) you will know.

Chapter Six

The Right Place—at the Right Time

A creature not too great or good
For human nature's daily food
For transient sorrows, simple wiles
Praise, blame, love, kisses, tears, smiles.
—William Wordsworth

Then the word of the LORD came to him: "Go at once to Zarephath of Sidon and stay there. I have commanded a widow in that place to supply you with food." So he went to Zarephath. (1 Kings 17:8–10)

On the move again.

The good thing about not having much is that there isn't much to pack. It's just a matter of hitting the road.

Elijah was traveling light, and it was well that he was. In a few short months, God transplanted his prophet from Tishbe to Samaria to Kerith to Zarephath.

The settled life is not necessarily the best life. It's not always good to be too long at ease.

"Moab," Jeremiah warned, "has been at ease since his youth; he has also been undisturbed on his lees, neither has he been emptied from vessel to vessel. . . . Therefore he retains his flavor, and his aroma has not changed" (Jeremiah 48:11 NASB).

Jeremiah was thinking of the process by which vintners made sweet wine. Grape juice was allowed to stand for a time until fermentation had done its work and the thick sediment had fallen to the bottom. The liquid at the top was then drawn off into another vessel. The pouring and settling process was repeated again and again until the wine was rendered fragrant and clear.

Change is unsettling but essential. It makes us sweeter, less demanding, less complaining, more willing to let go of what we want, more willing to do what God asks. We become more dependent on the peace of God for our tranquillity rather than on people, places, and things.

Change teaches us to put our roots down into God and find our resting place in him. Moses, who for eighty years had no place to call home, came to know that his only permanent dwelling place was nothing other than God (Psalm 90:1).

So Elijah, content to unsettle himself, set off for Zarephath in Phoenicia—a hundred miles away. It was a place that could only be reached by traveling across a land in which his name was hated and his life was in constant jeopardy. He had to elude the assassins working for Jezebel, hiding during the daylight hours, traveling under cover of darkness, always looking over his shoulder.

Zarephath, which he finally reached, was itself a dark and dangerous place. This was the Baal Belt, the heartland of that dark sect, under the shadow of Jezebel's formidable father, Ethbaal, whose dominion encompassed it.

Elijah had been sent to a very unsafe place. But then, no one ever said God's will wouldn't be dangerous.

"I am sending you out like sheep among wolves," Jesus said to his disciples (Matthew 10:16). God may indeed set us down in perilous places—neighborhoods, offices, fraternities, sororities, workshops, and classrooms where danger dwells.

You wonder—*What will happen to me here? Will I be suffocated by the darkness? Will my light be extinguished? Will the Spirit be quenched?*

The only way to know for sure is to do what God asks you to do and see what he will do.

One step at a time—
that's how we learn to walk.

Your first steps in such situations may be awkward and tentative—mine always are—but as you obey you will find the ground firm underfoot. You will be strengthened to take the next step and the next. One step at a time is all any of us are capable of. That's how we learn to walk.

But you say, "Suppose I take that first step. What will happen next?"

That's God's business. Your task and mine is to obey and to leave the consequences to him. This day's direction is all we need. Tomorrow's instruction is of no use to us at all. "We do not understand the next page of God's lesson book," MacDonald wrote. "We see only the one before us.

Nor shall we be allowed to turn the leaf until we have learned its lesson."

Our steps, Solomon assures us, are "directed by the Lord" (Proverbs 20:24). But what does that mean?

It means that

> if we concern ourselves with his will
>
> if we obey each day his directions
>
> if we heed each day his warnings
>
> if we walk by faith
>
> if we step out daily along the path of
> obedience as best we understand it

we will find that God takes responsibility for our decisions and actions. He will set us about his intended purpose. He will get us to the right person in the right place at the right time.

God's will is easy to find—if we *want* it. Really, the only people who miss his will are those who have no use for it. The months and years may show us that we've taken a strange, roundabout way, but if our hearts are right, our feet will never go astray. We will know what God wants us to do.

I cannot tell you how you will know, but I can tell you that when you have to know (and not necessarily before) you will know. Fifty years or so of walking with God have assured me that this premise is so.

Alexander McLaren wrote, "The one who is firmly settled upon this, 'Whatever God wants, God helping me I will do it,' will not be left in doubt as to what God does wish him to do."

And so Elijah went boldly to Phoenicia, just as he had gone to Samaria and then to Kerith. He was getting accustomed to doing what he was told. All he did, in fact, had one root: a willingness to obey.

Following Jesus means unending availability— to be expendable, if need be.

Following Jesus means a commitment to unending availability—to be ready, to be willing to go wherever we're sent—to be expendable, if need be. In words of a slogan I once saw on the side of a moving van: "Any load, any distance, any place, any time."

Unbelief always overwhelms us at the beginning of any uncertain enterprise. "Strong be the force," Yoda says, "but not *that* strong."

We're inclined to quibble with God for awhile, but he is wonderfully patient. We may talk back, complain, waver, worry, or run away when he asks us to do hard things, but if we will give him the chance, he will soften our wills to obey. He loves us too much to let us go.

Jesus taught:

"There was a man who had two sons. He went to the first and said, 'Son, go and work today in the vineyard.'

"'I will not,' he answered, but later he changed his mind and went.

"Then the father went to the other son and said the same thing. He answered, 'I will, sir,' but he did not go.

"Which of the two did what his father wanted?" [Jesus asked.]

"The first," they answered. (Matthew 21:28–31)

MacDonald captured the spirit of this hesitant obedience in verse:

I said—"Let me walk in the fields,"
*   He said—"No, walk in the town."*
I said—"There are no flowers there."
*   He said—"No flowers, but a crown."*
I said—"But the skies are dark,
*   There is nothing but noise and din."*
And He wept as He sent me back—
*   "There is more," He said: "there is sin."*

I said—"I shall miss the light
*   And friends will miss me, they say."*
He answered—"Choose tonight
*   If I am to miss you, or they."*
I pleaded for time to be given,
*   He said—"Is it hard to decide?*
It will not be hard in Heaven
*   To have followed the steps of your guide."*

Then into His hand went mine,
And into my heart came He,
And I walk in a light Divine,
The path I had feared to see.

It is the mercy of God that he demands our complete devotion. It is the way he gives himself to us. Time after time, saying no to God leads us into boredom and depression. Time after time, saying yes leads us into gusto and delight. We find the fullness of God by that oldest and oddest paradox of all: "Whoever loses his life for my sake will find it" (Matthew 10:39). No lesson is more clearly and consistently taught in this world.

Making the Connection

Elijah was willing to go to Zarephath or anywhere else God sent him, but he had a practical problem: How would he connect with the woman God had in mind? God gave no specific directions. She would not be holding up a placard like the limo drivers at the airport, nor would she be wearing a white carnation. It was a "puzzlement," as Winnie the Pooh used to say.

The prophet arrived in Zarephath hungry, thirsty, and spent after his hundred-mile hike. As he passed through the city gates, he spied a woman picking up sticks in order to prepare a meal. To some it would have seemed mere chance to find this woman here but not to Elijah. He believed in God's sovereign control of every element in his world; there were no maverick molecules in his universe.

Using a gambit our Lord later used with the Samaritan woman at the well, Elijah asked the widow for a cup of cold water, and the woman responded with kindness. Jesus implied that there was something in her that could not be found in any widow in Israel (Luke 4:25–26).

She had a soft heart in which the Word could take root.

He had found a woman uniquely prepared by God.

God searches everywhere, looking for honest, unadorned women and men—probing, delving, pursuing—intent on finding the faintest sign of desire. Anyone who wants to know God will be taught and thoroughly taught by him, Jesus said (John 7:17). He will see to it that they hear.

I think of a certain woman who sauntered down the aisle of an airplane on which Carolyn and I were flying. She was the consummate tourist—stereo headphones clamped on her head, camera strung on her neck.

"Is that seat saved?" she asked, pointing at an empty seat on the other side of Carolyn.

"Yes," I quipped, "for you," not knowing what a prophet I was.

In a few minutes, she and Carolyn were into a conversation about one thing and another, "Why are you flying to Boise?" Carolyn asked. Her simple question unlocked a torrent of tears. "To see my father before he dies," the woman said, weeping. She was looking for answers; God had prepared a place for her.

And then I think of a student on a California campus, sitting on the grass staring into space, whom I engaged in a conversation about spiritual things. He told me he was at that very moment thinking about God, about his grandmother's faith, and recalling a conversation in which a friend of his had explained the gospel. The love and prayers of a godly grandmother and the persistent witness of a friend had prepared the soil. God brought me to the right place at the right time to drop another seed into the ground.

Encouraged by the widow's response, Elijah asked the woman if she would prepare a meal. It was a modest request, but it unlocked the agony of her soul: "As surely as the LORD your God lives, . . . I don't have any bread—only a handful of flour in a jar and a little oil in a jug. I am gathering a few sticks to take home and make a meal for myself and my son, that we may eat it—and die" (1 Kings 17:12).

The woman was starving. She had only a handful of grain in a barrel, a little oil in a jar, and she was preparing to make one last meal for herself and her son and then die. She was living close to death and in great despair.

But what was her need to one whose mind was preoccupied with the presence and power of God? God had told Elijah that he would be fed by the widow, and so it would be.

"Don't be afraid," he said. "Go home and do as you have said. But first make a small cake of bread for me from what you have and bring it to me, and then make something for yourself and your son. For this is what the LORD, the God of Israel, says: 'The jar of flour will not be used up and the jug of oil will not run dry until the day the LORD gives rain on the land' " (1 Kings 17:13–14).

Elijah only needed to know that he was in the place God wanted him to be.

If so, God would take care of the rest.

"She went away and did as Elijah had told her. So there was food every day for Elijah and for the woman and her family. For the jar of flour was not used up and the jug of oil did not run dry, in keeping with the word of the LORD spoken by Elijah" (1 Kings 17:15–16). Each day, by faith, Elijah, the widow, and her son lived on their daily replenished stores.

In Phoenicia they said it was Baal who supplied one's meal and oil. He was the "son of dagon"—*dagon* is the Canaanite word for corn. He was also the god who supplied oil. It was said that when Baal ascends out of the earth:

> *The heavens rain oil,*
> *The wadies run with honey*
> *So I know that the mighty one, Baal lives*
> *Lo, the Prince, Lord of Earth exists.*

The widow did not know that Israel's God was the one who refilled the jar of flour and the jug of oil. The small supply of daily bread became the sign of God's goodness.

The family fare was frugal but sufficient for their daily needs. Elijah, I'm sure, would have preferred a *roomful* of sacks of meal and barrels of oil—but that's rarely God's way. His way is day by day.

Those who live like this—hand to mouth—are constantly reminded of God's love and their dependence on it. They are led again and again to the life of a little child, waiting each day for the Father's giving.

Elijah was just such a child: content to trust the living God, waiting for each day's gift handed to him out of that world next to ours, content to trust his heavenly Father who gives us all things richly to enjoy.

He knew that the responsibility for maintaining the little family rested wholly on God. That delivered him from anxiety and daily care. If God had guaranteed his support (and he had), it did not matter whether he could see the sources from which it came.

I'm reminded of C. S. Lewis's *Till We Have Faces*—his version of the Cupid and Psyche myth: Psyche, his young hero, lived in an unseen castle and ate at a sumptuous table that no one else could perceive. She had an invisible source of support.

As did Elijah: Each day God provided from his realm to Elijah's. Each day, the widow and her son observed Elijah resting under the shadow of God's wings. Each day, Elijah's simple life of faith was drawing this woman close to the heart of God.

But then—her world fell apart.

The widow's only son became ill, lapsed into a coma, and died. In her despair, the grieving woman lashed out at the prophet:

> *"What do you have against me, man of God? Did you come to
> remind me of my sin and kill my son?"*
>
> *"Give me your son," Elijah replied. He took him from her arms,
> carried him to the upper room where he was staying, and laid him
> on his bed. Then he cried out to the LORD, "O LORD my God, have
> you brought tragedy also upon this widow I am staying with, by
> causing her son to die?" Then he stretched himself out on the boy
> three times and cried to the LORD, "O LORD my God, let this boy's
> life return to him!"*
>
> *The LORD heard Elijah's cry, and the boy's life returned to him,
> and he lived. Elijah picked up the child and carried him down from
> the room into the house. He gave him to his mother and said, "Look,
> your son is alive!"*
>
> *Then the woman said to Elijah, "Now I know that you are a man
> of God and that the word of the LORD from your mouth is the
> truth."* (1 Kings 17:18–24)

This was a problem for which Baal had no answer.
One Canaanite myth speaks of that despair. It tells of an
empty promise of eternal life that the goddess Anat made to
a young man named Aqhat:

> *Ask for life, O Aqhat the youth;*
> > *Ask for life and I will give it to you.*
> *I will bestow immortality it on you;*
> > *I will make you count years with Baal;*
> *You will count months with the sons of El.*

The offer sounded good, but Aqhat knew better. He
had seen too many of his friends die. He answered,

Do not lie to me, O Maiden,
> *For to a youth your lying is loathsome.*
How can a mortal attain everlasting life?
> *Glaze will be poured on my head;*
Plaster on my pate;
> *And I will die as everyone dies;*
I will surely die.

Anat's offer was empty. Only "the LORD . . . makes alive" (1 Samuel 2:6).

It's characteristic of those who walk with God that they carry with them the spirit of life. They not only convince women and men of the truth of eternal life, but they are the means by which it enters into them. So it was with the prophet; so it is with us. Through us God can transform others, translating them from life to death.

And what was the result of Elijah's presence and quiet witness? The woman was drawn to God. In the beginning, she spoke of "the LORD *your* God" (1 Kings 17:12, emphasis added). In the end she entered into God's Word: "Now I know," she said, "that you are a man of God and that the word of the LORD from your mouth is the truth" (verse 24). This woman had been brought in.

I'm intrigued by her designation of Elijah as a "man of God." It's a phrase that bears intense scrutiny—particularly in the context of this woman's conversion.

The title suggests a towering, alarming figure, but actually a man of God is nothing more than one who is filled and flooded with God.

Moses bore the title. The compiler of the book of Deuteronomy wrote of the "blessing that Moses the man of God pronounced on the Israelites before his death"

(Deuteronomy 33:1). Thereafter Moses was called by that name (see Psalm 90:1).

Elisha was given that name by a woman in Israel who said to her husband, "I know that this man who often comes our way is a holy man of God" (2 Kings 4:9). Elisha had done no mighty works in her presence. He earned the title by his prayerful, godly character.

And the name was given to Elijah by the widow. As she observed his godly lifestyle day after day in her home, she began to think of him as a man of God.

Home is where we cast off restraint and let it all hang out, but Elijah was a different sort of person. He was as kind in small irritations as he was in crushing calamity, as humble and self-effacing with her child as he was in the presence of King Ahab, as patient over a glass of spilled milk as he was over the bitter animosity of Jezebel. He was one "around whose gate and garden children were unafraid to play."

Elijah ministered to the little family, taught God's Word, and lived it every day in their presence. His genial, patient, humble, honorable self-restraint in the midst of the incessant duties and demands of home life tugged at the widow's unbelieving heart. His calm, nonanxious presence in the face of adversity and death was a standing rebuke to her anxiety. His righteous character rebuked her ungodliness with hardly a word being said.

In the end her defenses crumbled.

Here's the remarkable thing: Elijah, Israel's great prophet, was not sent to square off with the king of Sidon but to board with a solitary widow in the little town of Zarephath. She was a Canaanite, a fact so offensive to the ancient rabbis that they contrived to represent her as a

disenfranchised Jew and made her out to be the mother of
Jonah. But it wasn't so. She wasn't a child of the covenant.
She was a raw pagan.

It seems odd to us that God would send his great representative across Israel to Phoenicia to find a solitary
woman and draw her in. But that's the way he is. He is not
willing that any should perish. He loves all people, great
and small.

I never read the story of Elijah and the widow in
Zarephath without thinking of Jesus' foray to this very
region. The two narratives are strikingly similar.

Jesus had withdrawn from Israel into Phoenicia, as
Elijah did, to the coast near the city of Tyre. He rented a
house there and settled down. By that time, Phoenicia had
lost much of her greatness, but her fierce pride and
immorality remained. It was a hotbed of hostility to God.

Mark reported that a certain woman intruded into
their all-male reverie. "Lord, Son of David, have mercy on
me" (Matthew 15:22), she blurted out. She had a severely
tormented child. She termed her daughter "terribly"
demonized.

Matthew described her as Canaanite, part of the native
population. Mark added additionally that she was a Greek
by religion. We think of the Greeks as cultured and refined,
and they were—yet their religion was essentially Devil
worship. Their word for divinity, *daimonion,* is the word
from which we get our word "demon," and Paul clearly
stated that those who worshiped the Greek gods of his day
were actually worshiping the Devil.

Perhaps this woman introduced her daughter to practices that led to her infestation. Her mother's heart was broken for her daughter—and for her own shame.

She made a terrible pest of herself—wouldn't take no for a negative. Her cries were persistent and pathetic, but, strangely, Jesus ignored her. That's so unlike our Lord, whose ears are always attentive to our cries.

His delay was for his disciples, whose racism and sexism had broken his heart. He tested them by saying, "I was sent only to the lost sheep of Israel" (Matthew 15:24). His disciples would have quickly agreed, disinclined as they were to believe that one like this woman could ever care about God.

But she did care about God. She had heard him calling from afar. She was one of God's lost sheep, whom Jesus said are "not of this sheep pen," but who "will listen to his voice" (John 10:16). This was a lesson in finding one errant sheep wherever it happens to be. Here in the story of the Syrophoenician woman we have another glimpse of the seeking, calling Shepherd: all are precious in his sight.

Jesus said to her: "First let the children eat" (Mark 7:27). The children, of course, were the children of God. Feeding them was Jesus' ministry.

"It is not right to take the children's bread and toss it to their dogs," Jesus said.

"Yes, Lord," she replied, perhaps with a twinkle in her eyes, "but even the [puppies] eat the crumbs that fall from their masters' table" (Matthew 15:27).

She had her eyes on her Master. *I may be a puppy,* she mused, *but I'm your puppy. Puppies have their rights.*

What audacious wit! "Was not that a master-stroke?" Luther said, "She snares Christ in his own words."

Jesus said to the woman "You have great faith" (verse 28). There were only two people in the world to whom he made that statement: a Roman centurion and this Canaanite. Both were outsiders.

"When the Son of Man comes, will he find faith on the earth?" Jesus asks (Luke 18:8). Yes indeed—in the most unlikely places and in the most unlikely people. He will find faith in those parts of our culture where men and women are tired of doing evil—and where even the good things of life no longer satisfy. Hopeless, they come seeking tenderness.

And God meets them!

It is his own decision, based on his choice, to pour out his love. He is driven by love not by their attractiveness. He is drawn to them—even (and especially) those who have done everything wrong.

"What do you think?" said Jesus, "If a man owns a hundred sheep, and one of them wanders away, will he not leave the ninety-nine on the hills and go to look for the one that wandered off? And if he finds it, I tell you the truth, he is happier about that one sheep than about the ninety-nine that did not wander off. In the same way your Father in heaven is not willing that any of these little ones should be lost" (Matthew 18:12–14).

Lost sheep are not doomed: they're the ones he came to save. "The ambitious, the vain, the highly sexed," says C. H. Sisson, are Christ's "natural prey."

There was a plaque that used to hang over my mother's desk. I saw it every day. It used to get under my skin, but then—it finally worked its way into my heart:

Only one life, 'twill soon be past. Only what's done for
Christ will last.

John Wesley said to his young Methodists, "You have nothing to do but to save souls. Therefore spend and be spent in this work. . . . It is not your main business . . . to take care of this or that society; but to save as many souls as you can; to bring as many sinners as you possibly can to repentance, and with all your power to build them up in that holiness without which they cannot see the Lord."

We must be faithful where we are—befriending one or two, if that's all we can do, loving them and imparting God's truth to them. As Francis Schaeffer used to say, "There are no little places and there are no little people." Every person in every place is of infinite value to God. "If there were only one of us," Augustine said, "Jesus would still have died."

"Who despises the day of small things?" asked one of Haggai's contemporaries (Zechariah 4:10). The answer, of course, is that we do. *Small* has fallen on hard times, inclined as we are to equate size with success. Small is now a value judgment: If we're limited to one or two, we're hardly worth anything at all.

Some years ago when I was involved in a ministry to university students, I invited a prominent Christian speaker to address a group of students on our campus. When only one person showed up he refused to talk to her. He was too big to speak to a crowd that small.

**Reality reveals itself
in quiet acts of mercy and goodness
that no one sees or applauds—but God.**

Some people look good with the masses but fail miserably when it comes to one or two. Yet our love for one person is the test of our love for all. Authentic Christianity is this: "to look after orphans and widows in their distress" (James 1:27). Reality reveals itself in quiet acts of mercy and goodness that no one sees or applauds—but God.

Think of our Lord—his lofty mission to save the world and yet his lowly manner. He always had time for one soul. Take Zacchaeus, for example. Zacchaeus had sold out to the evil empire and in the eyes of his own people had bartered his soul to the Devil. He had forsaken the way of the law and was on his way to gehenna. If he were in business today, he would be trafficking in illegal drugs or kiddie porn, but his heart was clambering for God.

No one took him seriously.

Except Jesus.

He knew the little man was looking for something.

Jesus picked Zacchaeus out of the crowd and invited himself over for lunch.

"Zacchaeus, come down immediately. I must stay at your house today." So he came down at once and welcomed him gladly. (Luke 19:5–6)

Jesus' self-invitation sounds presumptuous to us, but in his culture it was a gesture of acceptance. You only ate and drank with people you preferred. Zacchaeus knew that Jesus wanted to be his friend. And so it is. He was every sinner's friend: "The Son of Man came to seek and to save what was lost" (verse 10).

Zacchaeus, when he heard Jesus' offer, came down out of his tree to sit with him and listen to him. Later, he rose from the table to say, "'Look, Lord! Here and now I give half of my possessions to the poor, and if I have cheated anybody out of anything, I will pay back four times the amount.' Jesus said to him, 'Today, salvation has come to this house, because this man, too, is a son of Abraham' " (verses 8–9).

Zacchaeus had been brought in. The Son of Man had found one that was lost. He still has love for one person; he still sends his messengers after a single, solitary soul. As Meyer observed, "The mighty great cares about the mighty small."

Saving one is not a stepping-stone to greatness. It *is* greatness.

Edward Payson was a famous preacher of a bygone era. One stormy Sunday, he had only one person in his audience. Payson preached his sermon as carefully and earnestly as though the building were filled with eager listeners.

Some months later, his lone attendee called on him: "I was led to the Savior through that service," he said. "For whenever you talked about sin and salvation, I glanced around to see to whom you referred, but since there was no one there but me, I had no alternative but to lay every word to my heart and conscience!"

**"Who is my neighbor?"
The next person I meet whose deep needs
God exposes to my eyes.**

One or two is not too few; it's just about right. God saves people one by one. Size is nothing; substance is everything. So you only have access to one. *That* is your mission field. Saving one is not a stepping-stone to greatness. It *is* greatness. It's all a matter of perspective. We are not called upon to love the world and bring salvation to it. Only God "so loved the world." Our business, as Jesus made clear in the parable of the Good Samaritan, is to love our neighbors. "Who is my neighbor?" we ask. The next person we meet along the way whose deep needs God exposes to our eyes.

Our Lord did not have time to meet every need around him. There were many lepers in Israel who never experienced his touch. There were many widows and orphans for whom he had no word. He only did what the Father told him to do. He let God decide.

And so must we.

Ask God to bring you today to the one he has prepared. He will get you to the right place at the right time to speak to that person. He is prepared to dwell in your body, speak through your lips, work through your hands, and fulfill in you the great purpose of his will.

Recently Carolyn and I were flying from Frankfurt, Germany, to our home in Boise, Idaho. The the first leg was Frankfort to Boston.

It had been an exhausting week and I dropped off to sleep as soon as I found my seat, but I was soon awakened by a disturbance in the aisle.

The steward and a passenger who had been seated on Carolyn's left were arguing about the man's seat assignment. Somehow, he had been separated from his fiancée, who was seated several rows behind us.

The man grew increasingly angry and argumentative until another passenger, seated by the man's fiancée, offered to trade places. The swap was made and Carolyn's new seatmate settled into his place, drew out a legal pad, and began to work on some project.

Unfortunately, there was a garrulous little French boy seated on his left—a charming child—who wanted to talk. The man, who seemed to be the soul of patience, gave up his project after a few minutes and began to chat amiably with the boy. Carolyn was soon drawn into the conversation.

I heard the man say he was from Los Gatos, California, a town close to Los Altos, where Carolyn and I had lived for eighteen years. He was on the first leg of a flight to San Francisco. I heard Carolyn remark on the fact that we had many friends in the Bay Area, and then I went back to sleep.

When I awakened an hour or so later, I found Carolyn sharing her faith with her newfound friend, scribbling on his pad of paper, drawing diagrams, and animating her story. He was listening intently and asking questions. I sat there quietly and prayed for her and for the man.

At one point he said, "You believe as my wife does."

"Oh?" Carolyn replied. "And how did she become a follower of Christ?"

"Through Bible Study Fellowship," he responded.

"How did she find out about Bible Study Fellowship?" Carolyn asked.

"A friend of hers, Nel King, invited her to attend."

"That's remarkable!" Carolyn exclaimed. "Nel King is one of my best friends!"

And then the coin dropped: A few months before we moved to Boise, Nel had asked Carolyn to pray for a friend who had just become a Christian through Bible Study Fellowship and for her husband who was not yet a believer—the man now seated on Carolyn's left—there "by that power which erring men call chance."

Seeing Deeper

1. What is the spiritual danger of long-term comfort and stability?

2. "Change," writes the author, "is unsettling but essential." Changes don't always make sense from our point of view, because we can't see the end or the purpose. But the author says we need to cultivate a willingness to obey, that "following Christ means a commitment to unending availability." What's your typical reaction to changes that infringe on your comfort zones and upset your established routines? How could such changes be an opportunity to deepen your relationship with Christ and with his people?

3. Elijah was instructed by God to leave Kerith (south of Galilee and east of the Jordan) and go to Zarephath (far north along the coast of Phoenicia—now Lebanon). What do we know of Sidon (within ten miles of Zarephath) from 1 Kings 16:31? Putting yourself into Elijah's sandals for a moment—what would you think of this move?

4. Turn to the book of Jonah. In some ways, Jonah's experience paralleled Elijah's. Jonah was sent to Nineveh—the enemy—an idolatrous place. How did he respond to God's call to go? In chapter 4, why did Jonah become angry? What was God's reply?

5. In Matthew 15, Jesus withdrew to the same general area. A Canaanite mother came begging Jesus to save her daughter who was demon-possessed. Why did Jesus respond to her in such a seemingly coldhearted way? How does he respond to her answers?

6. God hates sin and rebellion but has compassion for those deceived by them and held in their grip. How did God describe Nineveh in Jonah 4? How did he react to the mother in Matthew 15? And how did he describe the lost in Matthew 18? How would you have described them? Do you find yourself responding more like God—or more like Jonah?

7. Look again at the widow of Zarephath. Read her statement to Elijah when she first met him (1 Kings 17:12). And now read her comment many months later (verse 24). We speak—others watch. We live—and our actions either confirm or negate our message. Have you given up on someone because she or he "didn't respond" to your message? Did it ever occur to you that this person might be watching you to see if your message rings true? In what way might this thought change your approach to relationships?

8. Who is your neighbor?

9. By the way—why would God have provided specifically flour and oil to the widow in Zarephath?

It's a simple fact that if you want to live a significant life you will be hated and opposed. Every step of the journey will be contested, every decision tested and challenged. Our Lord was despised and rejected. So you will be. "To be significant," said Emerson, "is to be misunderstood." The only way to avoid reproach is to be nothing, to do nothing, and to say nothing.

Chapter Seven

The
Troublemaker

Truths would you teach, or save a sinking land?
All fear, none aid you, and few understand.
                                        —Alexander Pope

*After a long time, in the third year, the word of the LORD came
to Elijah: "Go and present yourself to Ahab, and I will send rain on
the land." So Elijah went to present himself to Ahab. . . .*

*. . . When [Ahab] saw Elijah, he said to him, "Is that you, you
troubler of Israel?"*

*"I have not made trouble for Israel," Elijah replied. "But you
and your father's family have. You have abandoned the LORD's commands and have followed the Baals." (1 Kings 18:1–2, 17–18)*

In the jargon of newscasters, it was the "resumption of
hostilities."

In the idiom of sports reporters, it was "the ultimate
grudge match."

In one corner was Ahab the king, seething with hatred
for the prophet from Tishbe.

In the other corner was Elijah, God's representative, fully committed to do his Lord's bidding and to speak his Lord's message—no matter what. Now, after a lengthy separation, their paths were on a collision course.

Three and a half years had passed since Elijah's prayers had driven the clouds from the sky. One of those years must have passed at Kerith, another in Zarephath, before the widow's son was raised from the dead. For several months after, Elijah enjoyed a period of quiet rest.

He was being readied for his next step.

He was being prepared for combat.

While Elijah waited, the devastation he had predicted inflicted a terrible toll on the land. Pastures withered. Animals died. People groaned in misery. Yet there was no sign of repentance in Samaria—only a sullen silence.

As the drought worsened, Ahab searched both Israel and all the surrounding lands to locate Elijah to force him to withdraw his curse. In insane rage, Jezebel carried out her bloody pogrom against the prophets with ruthless precision—as though by slaughtering the prophets of God she could propitiate her own gods.

Yet the weary days ground on as before.

The sun rose and descended through a cloudless sky.

There was no sign of rain.

There was no kiss of dew.

There was no relief.

About this time, Jezebel left Samaria, perhaps taking flight to her homeland of Sidon by the sea to find relief. Ahab was left behind to mind the store and to stew in his own juices. In desperation, the king and Obadiah, his right hand, set out to survey the land to find a patch of grass for their starving donkeys.

They split up, each searching a different portion of the land. Obadiah stumbled upon Elijah, who was returning to Samaria. With Obadiah's reluctant complicity, Elijah arranged to meet with the king.

Ahab's opening thrust was timelessly characteristic of the man. "Is that you, you troubler of Israel?" he snarled. The king used a pronoun that suggests withering contempt. The very sight of the leather-clad man from across the Jordan sent Ahab into a blind, murderous rage.

Elijah's calm reply suggests he wasn't at all surprised by Ahab's venom and fury.

We ought not to be surprised, either.

It's a simple fact that if you want to live a significant life you will be hated and opposed. Every step of the journey will be contested, every decision tested and challenged. Our Lord was despised and rejected. So you will be. "To be significant," said Emerson, "is to be misunderstood."

The only way to avoid reproach is to be nothing, to do nothing, and to say nothing. Charles Briggs wrote:

> If your ambition is to avoid the troubles of life, the recipe is simple: shed your ambitions in every direction, cut the wings of every soaring purpose, and seek a little life with the fewest contacts and relations. . . . Tiny souls can dodge through life; bigger souls are blocked on every side. As soon as men and women begin to enlarge their lives, their resistances are multiplied.

There are always those
    who advocate peace at all costs
    who offer Band-Aids for bone-deep wounds
    who propose quick fixes that fix nothing

who choose only the path of least resistance
who preach peace, when there is no peace
who leave unresolved conflict and simmer-
    ing resentment in their wake

Should these "peace-seekers" be regarded as wise? No, for James tells us that "the wisdom that comes from heaven is *first* of all pure; *then* peace-loving" (3:17, emphasis added).

Jesus said, "No one who has left home or brothers or sisters or mother or father or children or fields for me and the gospel will fail to receive a hundred times as much in this present age (. . . and with them, persecutions)" (Mark 10:29–30).

Following Jesus means that you and I *will* be opposed. We will be assaulted, belabored, and disquieted. We will be maligned and misrepresented. Our motives will be impugned and our characters will be assassinated.

Peter said, "[Unbelievers] think it strange that you do not plunge with them into the same flood of dissipation, and they heap abuse on you" (1 Peter 4:4). If you try to live a worthwhile life you will experience malignity and hatred. Believe me, it's the name of the game.

We must not be deterred. We must not be derailed. Our detractors may hurt us profoundly, but we must not let them drive us away. We should see them as victims of the Evil One, whose sole purpose is to deter us from doing what God has called us to do.

"Even though much provoked," Abraham Lincoln said in the face of cruel and intense hostility, "let us do nothing through passion and ill temper. . . . Neither let us be slandered from our duty by false accusations against ourselves. . . . Let us have faith and in that faith let us to the end dare to do our duty as we understand it."

Acknowledging God's Part

The first step in dealing with hatred and opposition is to acknowledge God's hand in the matter. David said of Shimei's ruthless rock-throwing, "Leave him alone; let him curse, for the LORD has told him to" (2 Samuel 16:11). As the Heidelberg Catechism says, "All things . . . come to us not by chance but by God's hand."

Opposition and oppression can be God's voice speaking to us about some issue in us that must be confronted and put away before we can move on. "Truth is truth," MacDonald said, "whether it's spoken by the lips of Jesus or Balaam's ass."

"Consider the source," we say. No, we should rather consider the *criticism*.

We must listen to what God has to say. He may be speaking through our worst critics and enemies, pointing out some carnality or stupidity in us. "Consider the source," we say. No, we should rather consider the *criticism*. An old Yiddish proverb puts it well: "If one man call you an ass, pay him no mind. If two men call you an ass, go buy a saddle."

There is usually more truth in an enemy's words than in the counsel of our friends.

It may not be an easy thought for you and me to swallow, but there is usually more truth in an enemy's words than in the counsel of our friends. Perhaps our foes' eyes are sharper than our friends' eyes, or our friends may be aware of our weaknesses yet unwilling to tell us. Love is quick to note our faults, but sometimes slow to point them out and correct them. The highest love always girds itself for the task of washing our feet, but it's a dirty job, and our friends may be reluctant to roll up their sleeves and do it.

Spurgeon said, "Get your friend to tell you your faults, or better still, welcome any enemy who will watch you keenly and sting you savagely. What a blessing such an irritating critic will be to a wise man. What an intolerable nuisance to a fool."

> *We learn from our friends,*
> *But heaven knows,*
> *The lasting lessons*
> *Come from our foes.*
>
> —Pat D'Amico

We should listen carefully to our enemies and consider what's being said, giving the Holy Spirit adequate time to impress it upon us. We may respond by asking for time to think about what has been said. Then, if we are truly convinced of our sin, we should immediately confess it to God and to all those we have wronged.

If there is no basis for reproach, give thanks. We should be grateful that God has kept us from actual sin and thank him for his empowering grace. We *could* have committed the sin of which we are accused—or worse.

Ultimately, no criticism is undeserved. Though we may not be guilty of the specific sin of which we're charged, in one way or another, small or great, hidden or revealed, we are sinful to the core.

Boris Kornfield, the physician who led Solzhenitsyn to Christ, stated it like this: "On the whole," he said, "I have become convinced that there is no punishment that comes to us in this life on earth which is undeserved. Superficially, it can have nothing to do with what we are guilty of in actual fact, but if you go over your life with a fine tooth comb and ponder it deeply, you will always be able to hunt down that transgression of yours for which you have now received this blow."

There is an old story about Martin Luther and one of his detractors. It seems that Luther was approached one night and presented with a written litany of his sins. When he finished reading, Luther laid the list aside, sighed deeply, and said to the man, "Think a little harder. You've forgotten some." Would that God would grant me such humility.

But what can we say of those malicious people who are out to hang us? Is such cruelty the result of God's will?

Yes.

Indeed it is! Isaiah said, "It was the LORD's will to crush [his Servant] and cause him to suffer" (Isaiah 53:10). His bruisings and ours are part of our Father's good will.

Our Lord was nailed to the cross; you can count on being nailed to the wall.

Our Lord was nailed to the cross; you can count on being nailed to the wall. It's helpful to see each ordeal that way—as being crucified with Christ. Our hearts cry out, "Come down from the cross and save yourself!" But then we recall our Lord's words, "Not my will, but yours be done" (Luke 22:42).

God gives us over to such bruisings because they are part of the process to make us what he intends us to be. The hurting makes us sweeter, more mellow. We lose the fear of losing out; we learn to let go of what we want. We're not so easily provoked to wrath by harm or reproof. We learn to absorb abuse without retaliation, to accept reproof without defensiveness, to return a soft answer to wrath. It makes us calm and strong.

> *Firm in the right; mild to the wrong*
> *Our heart, in every raging throng*
> *A chamber shut for prayer and song.*
> —George MacDonald

Hostility and accusation teach us to pray—I mean *really* pray. David wrote, "In return for my friendship they accuse me, but I am a man of prayer" (Psalm 109:4). The translators supplied "a man of," but the text reads simply, "I am prayer." Prayer became the essence of David's life during those dark and hurtful days.

Opposition is a powerful instrument to develop our relationship with God.

Opposition is a powerful instrument to develop our relationship with God. It moves us closer to him and makes us more susceptible to his shaping. Thomas à Kempis wrote:

Sometimes it is good that we put up with people speaking against us, and sometimes it is good that we be thought of as bad and flawed, even when we do good things and have good intentions. Such troubles are often aids to humility, and they protect us from pride. Indeed, we are sometimes better at seeking God when people have nothing but bad things to say about us and when they refuse to give us credit for the things we have done! That being the case, we should so root ourselves in God that we do not need to look for comfort anywhere else.

We should accept every angry, hostile comment as an opportunity to draw near to God. We should look upon anyone who speaks against us as God's voice saying to us, "Come closer."

We can take shelter in the righteous judgment of God. "It may be that the LORD will see my distress and repay me with good for the cursing I am receiving today," David said of Shimei (2 Samuel 16:12).

When we reach the end of our rope, we must put ourselves in God's hands. He knows what others are saying about us and it grieves him far more than it grieves us. In time he will take our side. It's impossible for us to fully defend ourselves, and it's sinful to retaliate or take revenge. "This must be your retaliation," Rudolph Stier wrote. "Love and truth for hatred and lies."

We may ask our opponents to justify their charges, or we may meet them with steadfast denial. Truth spoken to establish the truth is not defensiveness. But when we have done all we can do, the only thing left is to wait patiently until God avenges the wrong and vindicates us. "Wisdom is proved right by her actions," Jesus said (Matthew 11:19).

The truth will come out in this life or in the next. Jesus—not our accusers—will have the last word!

Peter wrote this:

> *For what credit is there if, when you sin and are harshly treated, you endure it with patience? But if when you do what is right and suffer for it you patiently endure it, this finds favor with God. For you have been called for this purpose, since Christ also suffered for you, leaving you an example for you to follow in His steps, who committed no sin, nor was any deceit found in his mouth; and while being reviled, He did not revile in return; while suffering, he uttered no threats, but kept entrusting Himself to Him who judges righteously.* (1 Peter 2:20–23 NASB)

Jesus did not repay the world's curses and blows.

One church father, Justin Martyr, said, "Jesus' greatest miracle is that he did not retaliate." When our Lord's turn came and he was stretched out on the cross, instead of bitter resentment against his executioners he simply offered up his life to God.

That was the secret of Jesus' composure—and ours. We must take every criticism to our Advocate and let him vindicate us: "He stands at the right hand of the needy one, to save his life from those who condemn him" (Psalm 109:31).

We are shadowed and sheltered under God's wings. No one can hinder or harm us there. "Nothing in life is quite so exhilarating as being shot at without result," Winston Churchill said.

God says insistently and strongly: "[Those who oppose you] will fight against you but will not overcome you, for I am with you and will rescue you" (Jeremiah 1:19).

Note that God does not promise us lives free from attack. He only says we will not be *overcome*.

Here's a word that strengthens us when we are under attack and enables us to be nondefensive. The weak must defend their dignity and rights. Those who are strengthened by God can yield. "Let your gentleness be evident to all," Paul wrote, "The Lord is near" (Philippians 4:5). We will not be overcome!

Anxiety, intensity, instability, and pessimism plague us when we're on our own, but those who are shielded and strengthened by God share the calm and quiet nature of the one in whom they trust.

The wind of words may toss my heart,
But what is that to me!
Tis but a surface storm—Thou art
My deep, still resting sea.

So if my heart with trouble now
Be throbbing in my breast
Thou art my deepest heart, and Thou
O God, dost ever rest.

—George MacDonald

We unsettle ourselves when we try to defend ourselves. With Augustine, we should pray again and again, "Heal me of this lust of mine of always vindicating myself." Why do we smart under others' criticisms? Why do we care so much what foolish and sinful people say about us? Is it because we place too much value on our own reputations and on human favor and appreciation? Do we have a terrible fear of being despised and rejected?

"Let them talk," Alexander Whyte said. "Let them write; let them correct you; let them traduce you; let them judge and condemn you; let them slay you. . . . Oh the detestable passions that corrections and contradictions kindle up to fury in the proud heart of man! Eschew controversy as you would eschew the entrance into hell itself. Let them have their way."

We're *God's* servants. We report to him. And if he is satisfied with us, why should we break our hearts over what others say? The Lord of the Church has chosen us and put us to his intended task. He is our judge, and if he is pleased with us, there is nothing anyone can say or do that can ever dislodge us.

God is the only one who can properly evaluate the quality of our lives. He knows the latent forces as well as the patent facts. Paul could say, "I care very little if I am judged by you or by any human court; indeed I do not even judge myself. . . . It is the Lord who judges me" (1 Corinthians 4:3–4).

Ultimately, we are answerable to our Lord.

What to Do with Our Critics

We should forgive our critics from the heart. Jesus said, "Love your enemies, do good to those who hate you, bless those who curse you, pray for those who mistreat you" (Luke 6:27–28). Love, generosity, blessing, and intercessory prayer are the gifts we must give to those who revile us.

Consider Jesus' love for Judas. Though our Lord knew from the beginning who would betray him, not one of his disciples knew (John 13:22). Nothing in Jesus' behavior ever betrayed the betrayer.

Jesus prayed from the cross, "Father forgive them" (Luke 23:34)—not when the crucifying was over but at the very moment it was being done! So it must be for those of us who follow him.

"To see that my adversary gives me my rights is natural," Oswald Chambers wrote, "but from our Lord's standpoint it does not matter if I am defrauded or not; what does matter is that I do not defraud."

We must go beyond forgiveness to tender love—concerning ourselves more with the misery of the heart from which the hard words came than with the wrongs we've received. We must show our critics mercy, serve them, earnestly pray for them, and refuse to wrong them or withdraw from them. In the end, we must take their wrongs as God takes ours. Brooding over wrongs keeps the wounds open. Only forgiveness heals.

Impossible? "Nothing is impossible with God" (Luke 1:37). We should pray as MacDonald did: "O God, make me into a rock which swallows up the waves of wrong in its great caverns and never throws them back to swell the commotion of the angry sea from whence they came. Ah! To annihilate wrong in this way—to say, 'It shall not be wrong against me, so utterly do I forgive it!' "

This is the majesty of meekness: to keep our mouths closed and our hearts open when we're in the presence of our detractors.

This is the majesty of meekness: to bear patiently the spiteful attacks of malice and envy, to overcome evil with good, to live in the midst of difficult people and love them, to keep our mouths closed and our hearts open when we're in the presence of our detractors, to go unruffled and composed through a storm of unkindness and misrepresentation. This is only possible to those "in whose breast the dove-like Spirit has found an abiding place, and whose hearts are sentinelled by the peace of God. These are those who bear themselves as heroes in the fight" (Oswald Chambers).

Seeing Deeper

1. What are the two sides of the coin in becoming a Christian? See Mark 10:29–30.

2. What's the alternative to being criticized? Can we be used by God that way?

3. The author gives us uncomfortable counsel when he says: "There is usually more truth in an enemy's words than in the counsel of our friends." Why might that be so?

   a. Why do we resist criticism so strongly?

   b. What if every criticism caused us to turn to God and ask, "Is it so?" How might that change our reaction to criticism? to the critic?

4. Augustine prayed, "Heal me of this lust of mine of always vindicating myself." God seems not nearly so concerned with our circumstances as he is with our _____ to our circumstances.

a. Can we possibly defend ourselves against all criticism? Ought we to?

b. Can we assume most criticism is inaccurate and undeserved?

c. How can we condition ourselves to respond to it in a more effective and productive way?

5. "Pain tenderizes." How?

6. When we quickly defend ourselves from criticism, what character traits might we expect to exhibit? When we quietly accept and carefully consider criticism, what character traits might we exhibit?

What example has God given us? See 1 Peter 2:20–23.

"I got a putt, a pad, and an old lady," he said, "but I ain't got no peace." He spoke for all. Most men and women live lives of quiet desperation. But that's where we come in! It is our happy task to point out that every human desire is nothing less than a desire for God. Every impulse, every longing, every lust, every cry of the heart is but a cry after him. "Even when men knock on the door of a brothel," Chesterton said, "they are looking for God." We are born for God's love and nothing else will do.

Chapter Eight

When the Half-Gods Go

I heartily know
When half-gods go,
the gods arrive.
— Ralph Waldo Emerson

When Elijah left Zarephath he didn't have a clue.

No strategy. No crib sheet. No contingency plan. He had no idea where he was going or what he would say when he got there.

All the prophet knew was that he was to present himself to Ahab. That was it. Yet as he made his way toward that fateful rendezvous, the germ of an idea began to form in his mind.

I don't know if you've noticed or not, but God doesn't give us a thousand pieces to work with all at once. He doesn't dump the puzzle on the table in a jumbled pile. We would be much too confused by the clutter. No, like a parent helping a small child, he hands us one piece at a time. (And sometimes an edge piece to get us going.)

157

When prophet and king finally came together, Elijah knew exactly what he was to do. He said to Ahab:

"Now summon the people from all over Israel to meet me on Mount Carmel. And bring the four hundred and fifty prophets of Baal and the four hundred prophets of Asherah, who eat at Jezebel's table."

So Ahab sent word throughout all Israel and assembled the prophets on Mount Carmel. (1 Kings 18:19–20)

The fifteen minutes of fame Andy Warhol promised all of us was about to visit Elijah on the barren peak of Mount Carmel. Carmel was his moment in the sun, his magnum opus, his crowning day.

Elijah told the king only what he needed to know—enough to secure his cooperation. Ahab probably would have been highly uncooperative—apart from the desperate need for blessed rain.

Some system of communication must have existed throughout Israel that enabled the king to summon his people to this national referendum. Doubtless it took several days. During the interval, Elijah traveled to the mountain where he and his servant waited for the people to gather—and he prayed for the unfolding of the purposes of God.

Finally the day arrived. Picture the scene: It's early morning. Elijah stands on the highest point of the mountain—fourteen hundred feet above the plain below. *Kerem-El*, the ancient Canaanites named it: "the vineyard of [the god] El." It was an ancient high and holy place, long associated with the worship and religious rites of the Canaanites. The grandeur of Carmel filled the inhabitants of the land with awe.

To the west Elijah could see the white sails of
Phoenician ships as they left the port of Tyre. To the north
the sun was reflecting off the snow fields on the slopes of
Mount Hermon. At Carmel's base he could see the Kishon
River flowing through the plain of Esdraelon on its way to
the sea. To the east through the haze he could barely make
out the city of Jezreel, Ahab's summer residence, and the
towers of Jezebel's house of Baal.

Thousands of Israelites were gathering and taking up
positions from which they could watch the proceedings.
Ahab was borne to the front on a litter, with great pomp
and ceremony, surrounded by his cabinet and cadre and the
four hundred fifty prophets of Baal. (The queen and her
four hundred ladies of Asherah were AWOL. Apparently,
the independent-minded Jezebel defied the command of
the king.) Here and there among the crowd Elijah had his
sympathizers, but most of the faces were stone hard. They
were looking at a dead man.

Elijah had no backup, no friend in the court, no
Obadiah to bail him out. He could expect no better treat-
ment than that given to the other prophets whom Jezebel
had massacred.

The prophet stood alone.

One man against a nation.

But Elijah had a secret.

He was backed up by teeming millions of angels who
filled the heavens with their horses and chariots of fire. He
commanded the armies of God. This day, the man from
Tishbe would join those who "through faith conquered
kingdoms, administered justice, and gained what was
promised; who shut the mouths of lions, quenched the fury
of the flames, and escaped the edge of the sword; whose

weakness was turned to strength; and who became powerful in battle and routed foreign armies" (Hebrews 11:33–34). Nothing would be impossible for Elijah for nothing is impossible with God.

I recall stern Athanasius, the early church leader who tangled with the Holy Roman Empire over the issue of the person of Christ. Much hung in the balance: Was Jesus *homousias:* of the same substance with God, as Athanasius said, or merely *homoiousias:* of like substance with God, as Arius, Athanasius's opponent said? Some thought the argument silly, nothing more than semantics. Athanasius, after all, was quibbling over an iota, the smallest letter in the Greek alphabet.

But the issue was much more profound: Was Jesus God—or merely a godlike man? The world was turning to Arius; Athanasius, like lonely Elijah silhouetted against the top of Carmel, stood against the world.

When Athanasius appeared before the emperor to make his plea, the emperor shouted, "Athanasius, you pertinacious old man, don't you know the whole world is against you?"

"Then," Athanasius replied, "I am against the whole world."

Our safety does not lie in keeping ourselves safe. No, our safety lies in the center of God's will.

"Fear of man will prove to be a snare," the wise man says. "but whoever trusts in the LORD is kept safe"

(Proverbs 29:25). Our safety does not lie in keeping ourselves safe. No, our safety lies in knowing that we are in the
center of God's will. If so, we are in the safest place in the
world. No one can harm or hinder us there.

Oh, yes, they may kill you, but they can't really hurt
you. As Jesus said with such fine irony, "They will put some
of you to death. . . . But not a hair of your head will perish"
(Luke 21:16, 18).

Elijah, ever a man of few words, "went before the people and said, 'How long will you waver between two opinions? If the LORD is God, follow him; but if Baal is God, follow him.' But the people said nothing" (1 Kings 18:21).

To Elijah's mind there was no "if." He never doubted
for a moment that Yahweh was God. But he wanted the people to know that Baalism and Yahwism could never coexist.
There was no room for tolerance and diversity on this issue.
The two faiths were mutually, eternally contradictory. One
of them must be wrong. The time had come to choose.

"The people said nothing." They had nothing to say in
the face of Elijah's boldness—yet they must have known in
their hearts he was right. Guilty consciences make cowards
of us all.

> *Then Elijah said to them, "I am the only one of the LORD's
> prophets left, but Baal has four hundred and fifty prophets. Get two
> bulls for us. Let them choose one for themselves, and let them cut it
> into pieces and put it on the wood but not set fire to it. I will pre-
> pare the other bull and put it on the wood but not set fire to it.
> Then you call on the name of your god, and I will call on the name
> of the LORD. The god who answers by fire—he is God."*
>
> *Then all the people said, "What you say is good."* (verses
> 22–24)

Elijah laid down a challenge—an ordeal by fire: "The god who answers by fire—he is God." It was a fair proposal. The priests and the people looked at each other and nodded gravely: "What you say is good."

Baal, after all, was known as the god who answered by fire. It was reputed to be his specialty. He was the one, it was said, who generated the fire and storm that brought rain and fertility to the soil. Ugaritic sources reinforce the picture:

> He [Baal] throws flashes [of lightening] to the earth.

But Yahweh is the real God of fire. Fire symbolizes his holiness, his righteous judgment, his very presence. Every Israelite could recall occasions in the past when God had answered by fire.

His fire burned in the bush from which he called Moses, it shone over Israel in the wilderness, it flamed out from Sinai, it fell and smote the murmuring crowds, it fell on the sacrifice on the brazen altar. Flaming fire was the emblem of Yahweh, his calling card.

And so the lines were drawn.

> *Elijah said to the prophets of Baal, "Choose one of the bulls and prepare it first, since there are so many of you. Call on the name of your god, but do not light the fire." So they took the bull given them and prepared it.*
>
> *Then they called on the name of Baal from morning till noon. "O Baal, answer us!" they shouted. But there was no response; no one answered. And they danced around the altar they had made.*
> (verses 25–26)

Baal came up woefully short—didn't even put in an appearance. As Scripture says so succinctly, "There was no response; no one answered."

That's the way it is with the other gods. They never come through. The psalmist saw the crux when he wrote:

> *[Idols] have mouths, but cannot speak,*
> > *eyes, but they cannot see;*
> *they have ears, but cannot hear,*
> > *noses, but they cannot smell;*
> *they have hands, but cannot feel,*
> > *feet, but they cannot walk;*
> > *nor can they utter a sound with their throats.*
> *Those who make them will be like them,*
> > *and so will all who trust in them.*

—Psalm 115:5–8

The other gods are dead and so are those who worship them.

Three hours passed. Elijah began to bedevil them. Can't you visualize him walking about viewing the proceedings, shaking his head, rolling his eyes, stroking his grizzled beard?

"Shout louder!" he said. "Surely he is a god! Perhaps he is deep in thought, or busy, or traveling. Maybe he is sleeping and must be awakened." (1 Kings 18:27)

Irony dripped from his words. Was he playing to the audience of watching Israelites? Were there any chuckles in the gallery? It was characteristic of the prophets to poke fun at idols. They thought the whole idea of idols absurd and made up whimsical names for them: *"Gillul"* (little dung balls), they called them.

The ridicule is entirely appropriate: How absurd to think that something made by humans and designed for obsolescence could ever come through! Find meaning in a piece of heavy metal! C'mon, man, you've got to be kidding. *"Gillul,"* the prophets would say.

Goaded by Elijah's scorn:

[The prophets of Baal] shouted louder and slashed themselves with swords and spears, as was their custom, until their blood flowed. Midday passed, and they continued their frantic prophesying until the time for the evening sacrifice. But there was no response, no one answered, no one paid attention.

Then Elijah said to all the people, "Come here to me." They came to him, and he repaired the altar of the LORD, which was in ruins. Elijah took twelve stones, one for each of the tribes descended from Jacob, to whom the word of the LORD had come, saying, "Your name shall be Israel." With the stones he built an altar in the name of the LORD. (verses 28–32)

Elijah asked the people to draw near. He invited their scrutiny. They could see he had nothing up his sleeve—no hidden fire, no secret spark. (The prophets of Baal were noted for their chicanery.)

The prophet sought the original twelve stones that Jezebel's priests had scattered over the top of the mountain. He gathered them and reverently placed them together as a symbol of God's people gathered in worship around one Lord.

[Then Elijah] dug a trench around it [the altar] large enough to hold two seahs of seed. He arranged the wood, cut the bull into pieces and laid it on the wood. Then he said to them, "Fill four large jars with water and pour it on the offering and on the wood."

"Do it again," he said, and they did it again.

"Do it a third time," he ordered, and they did it the third time. The water ran down around the altar and even filled the trench.
(verses 32–35)

It's unnecessary to make things easy for God.

He dug a furrow around the altar about four inches wide, arranged the wood, and cut the sacrifice into pieces. Then three times he had water poured over the altar until the wood and the offering were drenched, the ground around the altar was saturated, and the furrows were brimming with water. I suppose the lesson is this: it's unnecessary to make things easy for God.

Then, at the time of the evening sacrifice in Jerusalem when the lamb was about to be offered up to God, Elijah stepped forward and prayed:

O LORD, God of Abraham, Isaac and Israel, let it be known today that you are God in Israel and that I am your servant and have done all these things at your command. Answer me, O LORD, answer me, so these people will know that you, O LORD, are God, and that you are turning their hearts back again. (verses 36–37)

No hysterics. No frantic gyrations. No prancing and dancing. Just quiet, confident asking. Just the calm assurance that the God who had called him to this place would answer. The burden of his prayer was that God would vindicate himself—show himself to be God indeed and bring glory to himself.

This, too, is the heart of our Lord's prayer. "Our Father in heaven, may your name be respected and honored greatly, may your kingdom come, may your will be done on earth as it is in heaven" (Matthew 6:9–10, my paraphrase).

Whenever we forget ourselves and plead for God's honor—he cannot resist.

Whenever we forget ourselves and plead for God's honor—that he will be taken seriously by our friends in the world—he cannot resist. We can win anything from him. Our Lord in his incarnation had but one passion: " 'Father, glorify your name!'

Then a voice came from heaven, 'I have glorified it, and will glorify it again' " (John 12:28).

On top of Mount Carmel, the result was the same.

Then the fire of the LORD fell and burned up the sacrifice, the wood, the stones and the soil, and also licked up the water in the trench.

When all the people saw this, they fell prostrate and cried, "The LORD, he is God! The LORD—he is God!" (1 Kings 18:38–39)

Our God is a consuming fire!

Carmel is one of those brief moments in history when God steps out of his unseen realm and makes his presence known. On this occasion there was no question who had the firepower. There was no place for a second opinion, no need to discuss it in the media or debate it on a TV talk show. The issue was *settled*.

Then Elijah commanded them, "Seize the prophets of Baal.
Don't let anyone get away!" They seized them and Elijah had
them brought down to the Kishon Valley and slaughtered there.
(verse 40)

It was a terrible act, yet what could Elijah do? To turn the prophets loose would be to invite a return to apostasy. There could be no compromise.

Realizing how cruelly they had been deceived, the people had a mind to obey. Closing ranks around the counterfeit priests, they escorted them down the mountain—and into eternity. Thus ended the bloody business of the day.

Elijah said to the shell-shocked Ahab, "Go, eat and drink, for there is the sound of a heavy rain." So Ahab went off to Samaria, while "Elijah climbed to the top of Carmel, bent down to the ground and put his face between his knees" (verses 41–42).

Elijah spent the evening in prayer. Though rain was near, he knew that his prayers were the means by which he would collaborate with God in bringing blessing to the land. Once more he persevered in prayer.

"Go and look toward the sea," he told his servant. And he went
up and looked.
"There is nothing there," he said.
Seven times Elijah said, "Go back."
The seventh time the servant reported, "A cloud as small as a
man's hand is rising from the sea."

So Elijah said, "Go and tell Ahab, 'Hitch up your chariot and go down before the rain stops you.'" (verses 43–44)

The servant went seven times and each time reported, "There is nothing there," yet Elijah continued to pray. How often our prayers return the same answer: There is no change, no sign of deliverance. "There is nothing there." And so we're inclined to give up. We do not know that God's answer is on the way.

Long before Elijah began his prayer vigil on the mountaintop—for weeks and months—the sun had been gathering up the mists from the Mediterranean and forming them into clouds. And now the wind was driving them inland toward Israel. "Before they call I will answer; while they are still speaking I will hear" (Isaiah 65:24).

Elijah was a man just like us. He prayed earnestly that it would not rain, and it did not rain on the land for three and a half years. Again he prayed, and the heavens gave rain, and the earth produced its crops. (James 5:17–18)

Thus Elijah—one solitary person—turned a nation away from false worship and back to the living and true God.

Idolatry Ain't What It Used to Be

Ancient idolatry was simple and direct: dancing around the altars of Baal, flirting and cavorting with the lovely ladies of Asherah. Present-day idolatry is more subtle and much more difficult to detect, but it's still with us: It's any devotion other than devotion to God.

John Calvin observed that human hearts are factories in which men and women manufacture gods. Money, power, sex, friendship, marriage, children, success, celebrity, enlightenment, travel, collecting, artistic creation, excess—these are the gods that those in our culture are inclined to treasure and to trust. Our neighbors are consumed by their interests, their goods, their getting ahead, but none of these things can satisfy the human heart. Eternity is written in the heart. Men and women are incurably religious—spiritual beings made in God's image, the most godlike beings on the face of the earth. They were made for God, and nothing else will do.

The idols themselves are nothing. Idol worship, however, is everything. It is "sacrifices . . . offered to demons" (1 Corinthians 10:20). Back of every human-made icon lies a spiritual being of immense power, playing on human hungers, sending women and men on fruitless quests for things that will not satisfy.

The Egyptians, for all their sophistication, wound up worshiping dung beetles.

Idolatry is Satan's way of diminishing the human race. Paul said of the idolaters of his day: "Their thinking became futile and their foolish hearts were darkened. Although they claimed to be wise, they became fools and exchanged the glory of the immortal God for images made to look like mortal man and birds and animals and reptiles" (Romans 1:21–23). The Egyptians, for all their sophistication, wound up worshiping dung beetles.

Idolatry demeans men and women—makes them less human and humane. They become enslaved to things designed to serve them. Their idols lead them around by the nose. "You know that when you were pagans, somehow or other you were influenced and led astray to mute idols," Paul reminds us (1 Corinthians 12:2).

God hates idolatry. He cannot let the objects of his great love be seduced and led away to destruction.

God hates idolatry. He cannot stand by and let the objects of his great love be seduced and led away to destruction. That's why he will not give up or go away until he has brought men and women to the place where they realize that their half-gods will never satisfy, and they turn from them to serve the living and true God.

Some years ago I penned these sentiments into my journal. They eventually ended up in a book:

> Sex is not the answer, no matter what they say. Where is this Great Sex, everywhere advertised, but nowhere delivered? Where is the romance and intimacy for which we long? It's ironic: the act that more than any other ought to assuage one's loneliness only intensifies it. Tina Turner belts out her poignant creed: "What does love have to do with it?" Eventually we too learn to get along without the complications of love.

Friendships don't satisfy. At least, they don't touch the deeper currents of life and love for which we long. "Even with the loved around me, still my heart says I am lonely," sighs some forgotten poet. Where is the human tenderness we seek—the readiness to love and accept? When we ask our friends to take away our loneliness, we force on them a burden too heavy for anyone to bear. They let us down or go away, and we go looking for someone else to curse with our demands. We are very difficult people. All we want is boundless love.

Parents never come through—especially our fathers. For some, the term *father* brings only blighted memories. They interpret the word by all they've longed for and missed out on in life. Even those of us who had good fathers often felt they weren't what we wanted them to be or needed them to be. We spent our growing-up years trying to win their approval, yet we never got the validation we sought. "There is never enough father," Robert Blye laments.

At my father's funeral a few years ago, as I stood beside his casket, Carolyn, speaking in her quiet wisdom, said to me, "It's too late, isn't it?" Exactly. Too late to gain his approval. A line from one of Len Deighton's books came to mind: "Do we never shed the tyranny of our father's love?"

Education yields only fragmentary results. We do time in various institutions, taking soundings here and there, but we never get to the bottom of things. There's so much labor in learning, so much to know that we cannot know. "I tasted wisdom," said one philosopher, "but it was far from me." That's the silent conclusion of everyone who matriculates. I think that's why there's so much melancholy on the campus.

Success is never final. The long climb from the bottom to the top of the hill is exhilarating. We play all the petty little games. We endure the privation, the competition, the demands, the drudgery, the long commutes. There's always one more deal to push through, one more rung to climb, one more achievement that will make us feel okay. We put in the time, we pay the price, and if we're lucky, one transaction finally puts us over the top, but what then? The top is never the pinnacle we thought it would be.

Money talks, but mostly it lies to us, deceiving us into believing that good fortune will bring us satisfaction and security. But having enough is never enough. Having more becomes the goad that drives us on. We pity the disillusioned, lonely old tycoon with his money fixation, but we don't learn the lesson:

> *Whoever loves money never has money enough;*
> *whoever loves wealth is never satisfied with his income.*
> —Ecclesiastes 5:10

"Fame is fleeting" are some of the truest words ever spoken. The fifteen minutes of prominence comes and goes. We may do something or say something that turns heads and causes people to stare at us for a few days, but we're soon forgotten. Emerson was right, "Every hero becomes a bore at last."

Marriage is not what it's cracked up to be. Despite the assurance of countless fairy tales, there's no direct causal relationship between getting married and living happily forever after. Couples start out well, but they fail because the emptiness and the ache of loneliness is within them where no one can touch it. Then for some desperate souls there are the *affairs*, to use the lighthearted term that we apply to such disastrous ordeals, and then there are the crude finalities: the divorces, the bitter custody fights, the demolition of once-happy families and the estrangement of the little ones who are left behind.

Children are a delight, and so are our grandchildren, of whom we grow so pesteringly fond. Our children offer us great happiness but also terribly hard work and at times great suffering. And then they leave home, as they should, and for some parents the empty nest seems to be more than they can endure. No, our children, no matter how much we give to them or they give to us, are not that final achievement for which we strive.

For many, *retirement* is the chief end. They spend their entire adult years trying to make enough money to retire, but having reached their goal they find it empty. Thoreau called it "destination sickness." There they are: exhausted from years of playing the game, well aware that time is running out. All the years spent worrying, scheming, maneuvering are now meaningless. You see them everywhere with that dead look in their eyes. They've arrived, and there's nothing left for which to live.

Then there is old age, with its failing pride and fading power—and regret. We're "hung by our history," as they say. We look back and see the past strewn with the debris of our sin. Yet there's nothing we can do about it. History, including our own, can't be changed.

The Rolling Stones were right: you "can't get no satisfaction." No matter what people achieve or acquire, there is always that thirst for something more which, as it turns out, is nothing more or less than God.

C. S. Lewis said, "If a man diligently followed this desire, pursuing the false objects until their falsity appeared and then resolutely abandoned them, he must come out at last into the clear knowledge that the human soul was made to enjoy some object that is never fully given—nay, cannot even be imagined as given—in our present mode of subjective and spatio-temporal experience."

Lewis puts it exactly right: our seeking is a stirring of absolute need—our need for God. As Augustine discovered, having searched almost forever for satisfaction in this world: "O God, you have made us for yourself and our hearts are restless until they find rest in you."

King Solomon was another individual who tried everything and found it wanting. Ecclesiastes is his journal—a record of what he describes as "chasing after the wind."

He undertook a project very few of us would or could tackle. He had the means and the time to test out every theory and philosophy of life: existentialism, idealism, realism, hedonism, epicureanism, you name it. He plumbed every depth, pulled up every root, turned over every rock, shook out every bug. Down through the years, he worked out the implications of every worldview and lifestyle, submitting each to brutal analysis.

In the end, he concluded that life was meaningless. "Vanity of vanities," he concluded forty times, using the Hebrew superlative to make his point. Everything adds up to zero—zilch. If this is all there is, the only thing left, as Bertrand Russell said, "is to build one's life on the firm foundation of unshakable despair."

Robert Ringer related the following anecdote:

In my early 20s I had the good fortune to be introduced to a wealthy old Wall Streeter. A *Wall Streeter* is used here as an investor who spends each day watching the ticker tape and maneuvering money in and out of stocks at hopefully opportune moments. Harold Hart epitomized a typical Wall Street success story. Struggling as a youngster, he was now a millionaire many times over. He had it all.

The biggie came one evening when I came to visit Mr. Hart to do a deal. When I arrived I found him resting tranquilly in his favorite chair, with servants waiting on him hand and foot. I sat there awhile waiting as he stared blankly into space. Finally he muttered, "You know, nature has played a great hoax on man. You work all your life, go through an endless number of struggles, play all the petty little games, and if you're lucky you finally make it to the top. Well, I made it a long time ago and you know what? It doesn't mean a damn thing. I tell you nature has made a fool of man and the biggest fool of all is me.

"Here I sit, in poor health, exhausted from years of playing the game, well aware that time is running out and I keep asking myself, 'Now what, genius? What's your next brilliant move going to be?' All that time I spent worrying, maneuvering—it was meaningless. Life is nothing but a big hoax. We think we're so important, but the truth is, we're nothing."

It's important for us to understand that life does not add up for unbelievers. When that truth finally sinks in, we begin to view the world of men and women differently. We cease to be intimidated. We lose our fear and awe of people.

Some years ago I befriended a young man who rode with a motorcycle gang in San Francisco. He had been raised among the Tarhaumara Indians in Mexico and was never able to adjust to life in the United States. One terrible night he was killed in a street fight in the city. Ron Ritchie, a friend of mine, and I conducted his funeral.

I've conducted many funerals in my time, but this was by far the most memorable. It was held at the gang's request in the Santa Cruz mountains in a natural bowl surrounding a small lake. Bikers gathered in their leathers and distributed themselves around us as we shared our gospel with them.

After the service a young man walked up to me, lowered his eyes, and muttered this unexpected line: "I got a putt, a pad, and an old lady," he said, "but I ain't got no peace."

He spoke for all. Thoreau was right: most men and women live lives of quiet desperation.

But that's where we come in! It is our happy task to point out that every human desire is nothing less than a desire for God. Every impulse, every longing, every lust, every cry of the heart is but a cry after him. "Even when men knock on the door of a brothel," Chesterton said, "they are looking for God." We are born for God's love, and nothing else will do.

There are two kinds of people we mix with every day. There are those who trip through life like Alfred E. Neuman with goof-grins on their faces, who, if they think about life at all, are more concerned about what it provides than what it means. These are the dear folks who sincerely believe that the secret of life is just enjoying the passage of time. They never think much about where they're going—or where it all will end.

Lewis's Screwtape, a demon briefing his demonic nephew on the way to seduce and destroy one of his clients, protests the nephew's use of reason and logic. He suggests that he befuddle him, distract him, get him to think that reality is nothing more than the stream of petty events going on around us. His method works with some—the man who comes home, puts on his old clothes, cracks a can of Coor's, flips on the TV, and flips off the world. He will know better someday.

And then there are those who spend their entire lives trying to discover what, if anything, life is all about. These are the serious seekers in this world, "who by persistence in doing good seek glory, honor and immortality" (Romans 2:7).

These are the lovers of music, art, and wisdom, who take on the ideas of all ages, examining them from all sides, trying them on for size, jettisoning some, embracing others, in order to find what is good and true and beautiful—always learning, always searching, always trusting that life someday will reveal its long-concealed and exquisite design.

Yet somewhere along the line—perhaps at midlife, perhaps when they are in sight of the end of their lives—the enterprise becomes utterly senseless. That's when they get deeply restless and the search for fulfillment no longer suffices. They get no satisfaction from the senses, celebrity, morality, artistic creation, a happy family, or any of the pursuits of the will or ego.

That's when they begin to despair. (Those who know so much and who have so much are often the ones who despair the most, it seems to me.) They despair because there's nothing left for which they must live, and the only thing they know for certain is that someday they must die.

It's then that they may stumble across you and me.

I recall a young hitchhiker I picked up one day—a graduate student in philosophy at the University of California at Berkeley. We chatted as we drove for a few miles, and then I asked him the question I often ask of new friends: "Do you have any interest in spiritual things?"

He turned in his seat and fixed me with a stare: "My friend," he said, "I've been looking for God all my life. Can you tell me how to know God?"

Diogenes, that cranky old cynic, spent his entire life looking for an honest man. Diogenes, I think, would have been pleased.

Seeing Deeper

1. Check out Isaiah 44:16–20 and Psalm 115:2–8 to see what Scripture says about idolatry. To our modern minds, bowing before an inanimate idol seems so foolish—so obviously futile. Present-day idolatry is much more subtle!

   a. What are the idols of today?

   b. What do people sacrifice to them?

   c. And how are people rewarded for their sacrifices?

2. Augustine said: "O God, you have made us for yourself, and our hearts are restless until they find rest in you." The author tells us that none of today's idols can satisfy the human heart. If women and men have this "God-shaped vacuum" in their hearts, why do they look elsewhere for fulfillment? Why aren't they more avid God-seekers?

3. The Evil One is called the Deceiver and the Father of Lies, while God is called the Way, the Truth, and the Life. Knowing this, why do people spend so much time and effort chasing the stuff of this world and so comparatively little time seeking after God?

   The author says, "Money talks, but mostly it lies to us." How do you see this being true?

4. In 1 Kings 18:21, Elijah made it clear that the worship of Yahweh and Baal could not coexist. Why not? Elijah said there should be a test, and the god who passed the test would be the true God, worthy of full devotion and service. That made sense to the people. Why doesn't it make sense to us? Why do we try to worship the Lord and our own pet idols at the same time?

5. Read Ecclesiastes 5:3. Have you ever become possessed by the desire for an object of some sort—something that constantly occupied your thoughts? How did you feel six weeks or six months after you acquired that object? Was it still the focus of your attention—or did thoughts of the next potential possession take its place? Discuss how much of life—resources and attention—gets consumed by this process. How can we escape?

6. "History, including our own, can't be changed." If we've been wasting our lives on the wrong pursuits with too little to show for it, nothing will change unless we make it change *beginning right now*. How will you respond to the next craving for something that offers temporary happiness? See Matthew 6:19–21.

7. Turn to Philippians 4:11–13. Why do you suppose Paul could say what he did? As you weigh the apostle's attitudes and priorities, what areas of your own heart need the most reconstruction?

The events we call tragedies, setbacks, and failures, are opportunities for God. He knows how to draw glory even from our ruin. The hour of deepest humiliation, when we feel defective and utterly disqualified, may be the hour that God uses us in unparalleled ways. Years of "wasted" effort may be the years when God plants an eternal harvest; though we have fished all night and caught nothing, the Great Angler is still double-baiting his hooks.

Chapter Nine

Beating the Blues

Is my gloom, after all,
Shade of His hand, outstretched caressingly?
——Francis Thompson

Entries in my journal:

October 9: It must be a blue Monday or a bad case of the blahs. I'm weary. Perhaps a good night's rest will set things right.

October 15: I have fallen into a very dark place. I wake up morning after morning gripped by melancholy, struggling to pull myself out of the gloom. It's as though I'm halfway up the side of a bottomless pit, hanging on for dear life, my handholds precarious, afraid to move for fear I will plunge into some dark abyss below.

November 1: Is my gloom nothing more than the "shade of His hand, outstretched caressingly"? Or have I done some awful thing for which I must now bear the consequences? I feel that I have failed miserably, let down those who relied on me.

November 12: Work is painful duty; people with problems are a bother; friends with sunny, cheerful dispositions are a special trial. I want to quit—get away from everything and everyone, take early retirement, build a cabin in the woods, get a permanent job in a lighthouse.

December 7: I care for nothing. I enjoy nothing. I can think of nothing to live for and nothing for which I am willing to die. Nothing displaces the darkness. Every day is a new shade of blue.

January 2: Yesterday was pure delight. It made me think that I might be out of the doldrums, but today I have slipped again into my old groove of misery. I can deal with the dreariness; it's the hope that is hardest to bear.

Even the best get depressed. Charles Spurgeon, John Bunyan, David Brainerd, Søren Kierkegaard—all suffered bouts of melancholy.

William Carey, that rugged old warrior, had his own dejections and defeats. On one occasion he wrote in his diary: "I am defective in all duties. . . . In prayer I wander and am formal. . . . I soon tire; devotion languishes; and I do not walk with God."

But of all examples, Elijah's depression is the most poignant. Here's a man who stepped directly from the wondrous heights of Carmel into a steep, black canyon of despair. Israel's historian recorded the story:

Now Ahab told Jezebel everything Elijah had done and how he
had killed all the prophets with the sword. So Jezebel sent a messen-
ger to Elijah to say, "May the gods deal with me, be it ever so
severely, if by this time tomorrow I do not make your life like that of
one of them."

Elijah was afraid and ran for his life. When he came to Beersheba
in Judah, he left his servant there, while he himself went a day's
journey into the desert. He came to a broom tree, sat down under it
and prayed that he might die. "I have had enough, LORD," he said.
"Take my life; I am no better than my ancestors." Then he lay down
under the tree and fell asleep. (1 Kings 19:1–5)

Exhilarated and adrenalized by his success on Mount
Carmel, the prophet "outran Ahab to Jezreel," a distance of
about twenty-five miles. As Elijah ran, illusions of grandeur
danced in his head . . . the death of state Baalism . . . a court
chaplaincy . . . legislative prayer breakfasts . . . another
opportunity to vindicate God's honor and make his mark
on the world.

But Jezebel had another idea.

Dream on, said Israel's murderous first lady. Then she
sent a messenger with this bit of terse verse: "May the gods
kill me/If I don't kill you/By this time tomorrow!"

Elijah's snappy rejoinder was to flee. "Elijah was
afraid and ran for his life." The text may also be translated,
"Elijah *saw!* He got the picture!"

Fueled by raw fear, Elijah picked up his heels and raced
all the way to Beersheba, a distance of about seventy miles.
The prophet's long-distance retreat makes the New York
City Marathon look like a jog through Central Park. When
he finally ran out of gas, he took shelter under a broom tree,
dripped from exhaustion, and prayed that he might die.

"I have had enough, LORD," he said. "Take my life; I am no better than my ancestors." *Enough, Lord! I'm a failure! I'm washed up! I'm dead meat! I quit!*

Elijah's comedown is classic: Overadrenalized, overextended, and emotionally depleted, brooding over his feelings of inadequacy and apparent failure, he collapsed into self-pity, withdrawal, and self-destructive thoughts.

Every one of us must stumble into such trenches along life's winding way. Sometimes without warning, discouragement creeps in silently on little cat's feet—like fog off the bay. Time and pain wear down resolve. Broken in spirit and bruised beyond repair, we get weary of soul. We ask ourselves, *What have I been spending my life for? Who is any better off from all my effort?* We find no pleasure or consolation in God or in his work.

These days bring with them an abiding sense of utter failure. Our yoke seems unbearable, our burdens heavy beyond endurance. And what makes our difficulties even more grievous is that we feel such terrible loneliness. No one seems to care. No one shares our outlook. Even God seems to shun us. And so, like Elijah, we cry, "It is enough!"

Sometimes our dark moods are nothing more than physical and emotional depletion. Like Elijah we've been running scared, overdoing everything, committing ourselves to more projects and plans than anyone could ever do. We try to be all things to all people all of the time. We string ourselves out, expending all our time and energy, adding our will to God's, trying to do extremely well what he never intended for us to do at all!

We overadrenalize our bodies, giving them no chance to recover. We give ourselves no margins in which to adjust to unexpected emergencies. Overworked and underslept, we finally reach our yield point, and we fold. Our bodies can't take it anymore. Unlike that battery-powered bunny, we just can't keep going.

Melancholy may be nothing but natural weariness. We're inclined to make something "spiritual" out of it.

It's good to know that our melancholy may be nothing but natural weariness. We're too inclined to make something profound or "spiritual" out of it, thinking that somehow we've gone wrong. We keep forgetting that we're only human, that "we have this treasure [Christ's divinity] in jars of clay [our humanity]" (2 Corinthians 4:7). The treasure is the only enduring element; the rest of us is frail and easily gives way.

We mortals should never trivialize our weariness. God doesn't.

"Fatigue makes cowards of us all," Vince Lombardi said. We start to lose focus and to lose our grasp on reality. We implode—withdraw into a state of self-condemnation and apathy. We lose concentration. We say things we would *never* say if we were fresh and well rested. We make unwise decisions based on feelings of inadequacy—and sometimes those decisions are irreversible. We mortals should never trivialize our weariness. God doesn't.

Elijah lay down under the tree and fell asleep.

All at once an angel touched him and said, "Get up and eat." He looked around, and there by his head was a cake of bread baked over hot coals, and a jar of water. He ate and drank and then lay down again.

The angel of the LORD came back a second time and touched him and said, "Get up and eat, for the journey is too much for you." So he got up and ate and drank. (1 Kings 19:5–8)

God understood Elijah's weary despair—and let him sleep.

Being spiritual may mean eating supper and hitting the sack.

Sleep is God's gift to his weary servants: "He grants sleep to those he loves" (Psalm 127:2). Being spiritual doesn't necessarily mean expending effort in contemplation and prayer; it may mean eating supper and hitting the sack.

God sent his angel to Elijah to touch him. No lecture, no rebuke, no chiding—only a gentle touch from one of the Lord's tender angels, awakening Elijah to find food and drink. He commands his angels concerning us, to keep us in all our ways (Psalm 91:11).

God finds us when we're down and out, when we have nothing left to give. He comes to take away our weariness. He never awakens anyone to disappointment but to the good things love has prepared.

John, who learned God's love on Jesus' breast, tells in words so simple and direct: "We know and rely on the love

God has for us" (1 John 4:16). I go back to these words again and again.

Perhaps the best way to know God's love is to experience it in times of declension and deep discouragement, when we feel most undeserving of it. "Your love is better than life" (Psalm 63:3).

Strengthened by food and rest, Elijah "traveled forty days and forty nights until he reached Horeb, the mountain of God. There he went into a cave and spent the night" (1 Kings 19:8–9). In the strength of God's angel food, Elijah journeyed into the wilderness to Mount Horeb (Sinai), the mountain of revelation, where God always spoke his mind. There the Lord addressed the deeper elements of Elijah's discouragement.

> And the word of the LORD came to him: "What are you doing here, Elijah?"
>
> He replied, "I have been very zealous for the LORD God Almighty. The Israelites have rejected your covenant, broken down your altars, and put your prophets to death with the sword. I am the only one left, and now they are trying to kill me too."
>
> The LORD said, "Go out and stand on the mountain in the presence of the LORD, for the LORD is about to pass by."
>
> Then a great and powerful wind tore the mountains apart and shattered the rocks before the LORD, but the LORD was not in the wind. After the wind there was an earthquake, but the LORD was not in the earthquake. After the earthquake came a fire, but the LORD was not in the fire. And after the fire came a gentle whisper. When Elijah heard it, he pulled his cloak over his face and went out and stood at the mouth of the cave.
>
> Then a voice said to him, "What are you doing here, Elijah?"
> (verses 9–13)

"The Lord is going to pass by," Elijah was assured, and so he looked for signs of God's passing. First came the hurricane blast of windstorm, so powerful it splintered the very rocks. As the wind died down, a mighty earthquake rumbled across the landscape. No sooner had the dust settled from the earthquake than a firestorm descended out of the clear blue, searing all in its path, devastating in its heat.

Yet in each of these mighty displays, God was conspicuous by his absence.

When he finally did pass by, Elijah saw nothing, felt nothing.

The only evidence of God was a still, small voice—a nearly inaudible whisper.

God's heroics are rarely as expected.

You never know about God. He may appear in extraordinary and melodramatic ways—in hurricane, earthquake, and storm. But that's not his typical style. He seems to prefer much less obvious, less theatrical methods. God's heroics, when they appear, are rarely as expected. He works in quietness, his Spirit gently wafting like the wind here and there, touching one, touching another, working in silence to get his work done. The obvious is usually spurious. God's best efforts are rarely seen. That's the word from Sinai.

The problem with Elijah was that he had wholly unrealistic expectations of God. He had seen the Lord manifest himself in stupendous display on Mount Carmel. He expected a repeat performance—that God would make short work of Jezebel, blasting her off the face of the earth with a fireball. But instead of a lightning bolt, Jezebel got God's forbearance, and Elijah got a contract on his life. It was more than he could process at the time, and the disappointed prophet collapsed into depression.

God's way of correcting Elijah's perspective was to bring him to the place of revelation, which is what he must do with us again and again. It's in that quiet place that we hear God's voice. That's where we hear the truth, the whole truth, and nothing but the truth. That's where we get our erroneous zones corrected; that's where we get real.

Folk Christianity—that perspective nowhere taught in the Bible but generally believed—says that everyone is a winner, no one gets Alzheimer's, no one dies from cancer, no one fails in marriage, no one falls to mental illness. Everyone lives happily forever after.

But that's not the way it is.

Life is difficult.

"The world is painful in any case; but it is quite unbearable if anybody gives us the idea that we are meant to be liking it," Charles Williams said. When people tell me that life is hard, I reply, *"Of course* it is." I find that answer more satisfying than anything else I can say. Every year confirms my belief that life is difficult and demanding and sometimes the harder tests are further along. Any other response is unrealistic.

Here I'm reminded of Roy Hobbs, the protagonist in the movie and novel, *The Natural,* and his memorable line: "Life just didn't turn out the way I thought it would." It rarely does. We lose our jobs; we lose our health; we lose our children, one way or another. Our stocks fall, our retirement plans fail, our dreams go belly-up, our best laid schemes "gang aft a-gley." We labor long hours with only fragmentary results. We're disregarded and ignored, slandered and maligned; we get trampled on by insensitive people. Some days we fall flat on our faces. Our best efforts are a disaster, our best foot forward becomes a bitter embarrassment. As my friend Fred Smith says, "Anything is possible with God—even failure."

But not to worry: The events that we call tragedies, setbacks, and failures are opportunities for God. He knows how to draw glory even from our ruin. "Not to be downcast after failure is one of the marks of true sanctity" (Dom Augustine Guillerand).

The hour of deepest humiliation, when we feel defective and utterly disqualified, may be the hour that God uses us in unparalleled ways. Years of "wasted" effort may be the years when God plants an eternal harvest; though we have fished all night and caught nothing, the Great Angler is still double-baiting his hooks.

There's more going on in heaven and on earth than we can ever know! Though we think our efforts have been in vain, there's something in the wind. God's Spirit is wafting about, deftly and tenderly touching others, touching us, making us more like him than we ever thought possible, using us to influence others in ways we never imagined.

Matthew Arnold has written:

> *We cannot kindle what we will*
> *The fire which in the heart resides;*
> *The Spirit bloweth and is still,*
> *In mystery our soul abides.*
> *But tasks in hours of insight will'd*
> *Can be through hours of gloom fulfilled.*

With aching hands and bleeding feet
We dig and heap, lay stone on stone;
We bear the burden and the heat
Of the long day and wish 'twere done
Not till the hours of light return,
All we have built do we discern.

The Suffering Servant

It may surprise you to know that our Lord had his days of deep discouragement.

Peering down the centuries, Isaiah uncovered the heart of Christ during one of those dark periods of his life when he wanted to give up:

I have labored to no purpose; I have spent my strength in vain and for nothing. (Isaiah 49:4)

He had done what he was called to do. He had faithfully carried out his mission and—it was all for nothing! Or so it seemed. He had preached his heart out, extended himself, discipled and counseled faithfully—and for what? To be despised and rejected. The crowds were turning off, his disciples were disenchanted and drifting away.

But then, the Lord said to our Lord, "It is too small a thing for you to be my servant to restore the tribes of Jacob and bring back those of Israel I have kept. *I will also make you a light for the Gentiles, that you may bring my salvation to the ends of the earth* (verse 6, emphasis added).

The Servant thought his mission was to gather Israel (verse 5), but God had something greater in mind. He wanted the world—Russians, Romanians, Hungarians, Arabs, and Americans from Idaho. And he wanted men and women from twenty centuries or more. The Servant's rejection, though it seemed to be failure, was in fact a necessary component of that greater plan. That's what enabled our Lord to set his face like a flint and go to Jerusalem to be despised and rejected and to die.

Perhaps you've served a congregation faithfully only to be turned out in the end.

Perhaps you're a parent who has poured your life into your children only to have them turn against you.

Perhaps you've given your youth and your heart and soul to your marriage only to have your spouse walk away.

You've done your best . . . you've given your all . . . you've gone the extra mile—but God has not come through!

It's good to acknowledge our pain, just as the Servant acknowledged his. We're not stoics seeking to be pure of mind and to suppress all emotion. There's no virtue in the stiff upper lip. But when all is said and done, at the end of the day, at the end of years, we have no one to whom we can go but our Lord. As the Servant put it, "What is due to me is in the LORD's hand, and my reward is with my God" (verse 4). God is able to do exceedingly, abundantly above anything you could ever ask or imagine. He is at work, if not in the strong winds then in the gentle zephyr; if not in the earthquake then in our heartbreak; in crowds or lonely hearts; in multitudes that we see or in those like the seven thousand who were known to none but God.

The wind blows where it will. We can't control it; we can only believe that it is true. That's the perspective that Elijah learned in that quiet place; that's what we learn.

So let the noise subside,
And listen deep inside;
He will speak; he will speak.

But it won't be an earthquake;
And it won't be fire;
Or the whirling wind;
Taking you higher.
It will be a still small voice;
And you'll have no choice;
But to hear; but to hear.

—John Fischer

One Way to Get Going

Elijah missed the message: When asked again, "What are you doing here, Elijah," he simply rewound the tape and repeated himself, "I have been very zealous for the LORD God Almighty. The Israelites have rejected your covenant, broken down your altars, and put your prophets to death with the sword. I am the only one left, and now they are trying to kill me too."

The Lord said to him:

Go back the way you came, and go to the Desert of Damascus. When you get there, anoint Hazael king over Aram. Also, anoint Jehu son of Nimshi king over Israel, and anoint Elisha son of Shaphat from Abel Meholah to succeed you as prophet. Jehu will put to death any who escape the sword of Hazael, and Elisha will put to death any who escape the sword of Jehu. Yet I reserve seven thousand in Israel—all whose knees have not bowed down to Baal and all whose mouths have not kissed him. (1 Kings 19:15–18)

God's word was insistent: Go back! You still have work to do!

There were things of great importance for Elijah to accomplish: He was to anoint Hazael, the Syrian king who unwittingly became Elijah's ally in the struggle against Israel and Ahab (2 Kings 13:22). He was to anoint Jehu king over Israel, the man who eventually brought the evil Jezebel to her well-deserved end. He was to anoint Elisha, his companion in ministry and ultimate successor.

Furthermore, God assured Elijah that he was *not* alone. In fact, he was part of a significant whole, a faithful remnant much larger than the prophet had even dreamed. There were yet thousands in Israel—"all whose knees have not bowed down to Baal and all whose mouths have not kissed him."

Looking back on this whole account, I'm encouraged that even when Elijah couldn't master his emotions, even when he had no strength to climb out of his dark mood, not even God insisted upon it. Nor did God's patient word to his servant immediately take hold. As with Elijah, our emotions may be beyond our control. Black moods and the vice-grip of melancholy may continue long after the causes of depression are removed. Sadness needs its time to be.

No, Elijah wasn't asked to alter his mood, but he was asked to choose. He was asked to exercise that part of him that remained fully operative: *his will.* A century ago, British minister Francis Paget said this: "It may be impossible at times to feel what one would; it is not impossible to will what one should; and that, if the will be real and honest, is what matters most."

John White wrote:

There is no place for giving up. The warfare is much bigger than our personal humiliations. To feel sorry for oneself is totally inappropriate. Over such a soldier I would pour a bucket of icy water. I would drag him to his feet, kick him in the rear end and put his sword in his hand and shout, "Now fight!" In some circumstances one must be cruel to be kind. What if you've fallen for a tempting ruse of the Enemy? What if you're not the most brilliant swordsman in the army? You hold Excaliber in your hand. Get behind the lines for a break if you're too weak to go on and strengthen yourself with a powerful draught of Romans 8:1–4. Then get back into the fight before your muscles get stiff.

We can get back into the fight—if we will.

We can get back into the fight—if we will. And therein lies the rub.

And therein lies the rub.

Do we really *want* to deal with our discouragement?

Blue moods can initially be pleasurable; pandering to our misery and nursing self-pity feels good for a season, but like all illicit pleasure the aftertaste is bitter. Sowing to one's own flesh inevitably leads to corruption (Galatians 6:8–10).

Somewhere along the line, we must *decide* that despair must go. We must not be passive and wait for it to go away by itself. We must learn to battle fiercely against discouragement. And most importantly, we must stay near the place of revelation, sit at our Lord's feet, and listen to his words. He reminds us there of the things that matter:

        who he is
        what he has done
        what he is doing

It's there, at his feet, that we get his perspective. It is there we regain our focus. It is there we reestablish our priorities. In that quiet place we hear again the words so recently covered over by our pain: "The one who calls you is faithful and *he* will do it" (1 Thessalonians 5:24, emphasis added).

We must get up and get going. There's always something God is asking us to do, something as simple as fixing our faces or fixing a meal. He only asks us to do what he empowers us to do. We must shake off our lethargy and, like that other cripple whom Jesus restored, get up from our beds and *walk*. It's necessary for us to take that first step, for God "will carry us in his arms till we are able to walk and he will carry us in his arms when we are weary and cannot walk; but he will not carry us if we will not walk" (MacDonald).

Hard to do? You bet it is! Like plunging into an icy stream. But it can be done. When we choose to do his will, God gives us what we need to comply. Our feelings may lag, the dark mood may linger, but God will indeed carry us in his arms until we're back on our feet.

As Scripture affirms, "So Elijah *went* from there" (1 Kings 19:19, emphasis added).

He made his choice. He got back into the action. Will you?

Seeing Deeper

1. Please go back and review 1 Kings 18:16–19:18. Elijah confronted the king, defied the false prophets, gave proof that the Lord is God, prayed for rain, and was so

exhilarated he ran ahead of Ahab's chariot. Yet by
verse 3 of chapter 19, Elijah asks God to end his life!
Why? How did God respond to his servant? How does
God respond to us in similar situations?

2. Have you ever found yourself wondering, *What am I
spending my life for? Who is any better off from my effort?*
What were the circumstances leading up to those
thoughts?

3. The author suggests we often work too hard. We
attempt to do too much, seek to be all things to all people, and keep trying to do "extremely well what he
never intended for us to do at all!" Reflecting on your
own life a little, what are the first areas of your life to
suffer when you find yourself too busy, too pressured,
too stressed? How does God feel about your busyness?
What do you think his counsel to you might be?

4. The author writes: "We overadrenalize our bodies, giving them no chance to recover. We give ourselves no
margins in which to adjust to unexpected emergencies.
Overworked and underslept, we finally reach our yield
point, and we fold."

   a. What happens to our emotions when we fold? What
   do we tend to read into those down days? How often
   do we recognize our symptoms as physical exhaustion, and how regularly do we interpret exhaustion
   as spiritual failure?

b. When Elijah folded, what was he particularly dis-
   couraged about? Can you identify with him? What
   pressures in your life bring those feelings on?

5. When God showed himself to Elijah on the mountain, it
   wasn't in the rock-shattering wind nor the earthquake
   nor the fire—in fact his absence was obvious in those
   frantic scenes. He came in a "gentle whisper" and Elijah
   stepped forward at the realization of God's presence.
   Why a gentle whisper—or, as the King James renders it,
   "a still, small voice"? What does it say about how God
   reveals himself? What should it say to us when we can't
   see God working?

6. The author spoke of "folk Christianity." What is that—
   and what did he say about it? Why does he make the
   conclusions he does?

7. "Sadness," writes the author, "needs its time to be." But
   we're told, "rest, just don't sink." Explain what you
   think he means.

8. If you were to endure a period of depression in the coming days, would you regard it any differently after reading this chapter? What new perspectives might you
   bring to those inevitable down times of life?

It's the assurance that keeps us steady in the face of all the evil that men and women do. It's that unshakable truth to which we may cling as the enemy's shadow falls over our nation and culture. We can take evil seriously, but we needn't panic in the face of its steady advance. Why? Because we know that God's processes are perfectly adequate to deal with the worst that perverse and villainous people can do. That confidence results in poise in the face of appalling, disorienting disorder. You can keep your head when all others are losing theirs, because you do understand the situation.

Chapter Ten

The Other Side of God

There is a line, by us unseen,
That crosses every path;
The hidden boundary between
God's patience and His wrath.
                    —Joseph Addison Alexander

We see thugs, tyrants, and other terrible women and men getting away with appalling evil around the world.

We read the newspaper and shake our heads over depravity's inexorable advance through our culture, within our government, and through our educational systems.

Sometimes we wonder if God is minding the store.

Why doesn't he do *something?*

We ask the question because we see only one side of God—his mercy and long-suffering patience. But God's tolerance is not the whole story. He is wonderfully gracious, incredibly patient, and not willing that any should perish. But if a man or a woman continues to spurn his grace and patience, if he or she will not listen, will not relent, will not turn—there is nothing left but death—and after death the judgment. "They will have to give account to him who is ready to judge the living and the dead" (1 Peter 4:5).

Consider Ahab, who met his well-deserved end on the killing fields of Ramoth Gilead. It happened like this.

Ahab's army had caught a large Syrian contingent by surprise, besieged their camp while they were prematurely toasting their victory, and put them to flight. In a second battle they drove them across the Jordan.

Now the land could rest.

But not Ahab.

His ego was so deflated by sin he needed a string of additional victories to compensate. He had to have something more. As it turned out, that something more was a little plot of ground adjoining his estate. It belonged to his neighbor Naboth the Jezreelite—but Ahab had to have it. "Avarice," wrote Pope, "is the never-failing vice of fools."

> *Ahab said to Naboth, "Let me have your vineyard to use for a vegetable garden, since it is close to my palace. In exchange I will give you a better vineyard or, if you prefer, I will pay you whatever it is worth."*
>
> *But Naboth replied, "The LORD forbid that I should give you the inheritance of my fathers."*
>
> *So Ahab went home, sullen and angry because Naboth the Jezreelite had said, "I will not give you the inheritance of my fathers." He lay on his bed sulking and refused to eat.* (1 Kings 21:2–4)

On the surface Ahab's request seemed reasonable. He didn't conscript the land as other Oriental kings might have done. He offered to buy it or swap for some better place.

Naboth, however, had no desire to part with his ancestral inheritance. It was the law in Israel that everyone had perpetual right to a personal piece of ground and no one—not even the king—could force an Israelite to part with that asset. Naboth had deep roots in his family's property, and those roots meant more to him than money or mere acreage.

Ahab stalked off to his chariot and went back to Jezreel, where he went into a funk—"he lay on his bed sulking and refused to eat." Scheming, manipulating little man, making much of trifles and thinking only of himself. He knew very well his peevishness would bring the murderous Jezebel into play.

> *His wife Jezebel came in and asked him, "Why are you so sullen? Why won't you eat?"*
>
> *He answered her, "Because I said to Naboth the Jezreelite, 'Sell me your vineyard; or if you prefer, I will give you another vineyard in its place.' But he said, ' I will not give you my vineyard.' "*
>
> *Jezebel his wife said, "Is this how you act as king over Israel? Get up and eat! Cheer up. I'll get you the vineyard of Naboth the Jezreelite." (21:5–7)*

"Is this any way for a king to act?" Jezebel sneered. "What are you—a man or a mouse? Squeak up! Get out of bed and go back to work. I'll get you your dinky little vineyard."

And so she did. Jezebel was a woman of determination and means.

> *She wrote letters in Ahab's name, placed his seal on them, and sent them to the elders and nobles who lived in Naboth's city with him. In those letters she wrote:*
>
> *"Proclaim a day of fasting and seat Naboth in a prominent place among the people. But seat two scoundrels [sons of Belial—'thugs']*

opposite him and have them testify that he has cursed both God and
the king. Then take him out and stone him to death."

So the elders and nobles who lived in Naboth's city did as Jezebel
directed in the letters she had written to them. (21:8–11)

In a few more days, the deed was done. The town
fathers who long before had sold out to Jezebel trumped up
charges of insurrection and blasphemy against Naboth,
suborned the testimony of a couple of goons, and with one
stroke secured the judicial murder of this good man, his
sons, and heirs (see 2 Kings 9:26).

As soon as Jezebel heard that Naboth had been stoned to death,
she said to Ahab, "Get up and take possession of the vineyard of
Naboth the Jezreelite that he refused to sell you. He is no longer
alive, but dead" [literally: "he has died"]. When Ahab heard that
Naboth was dead, he got up and went down to take possession of
Naboth's vineyard. (1 Kings 21:15–16)

Naboth's vineyard reverted to the crown. Ahab had
his vegetable garden.

Then the word of the LORD came to Elijah the Tishbite: "Go
down to meet Ahab king of Israel, who rules in Samaria. He is now
in Naboth's vineyard, where he has gone to take possession of it.
Say to him, 'This is what the LORD says: Have you not murdered a
man and seized his property?' Then say to him, 'This is what the
LORD says: In the place where dogs licked up Naboth's blood, dogs
will lick up your blood—yes, yours!' "

Ahab said to Elijah, "So you have found me, my enemy!"

"I have found you," he answered, "because you have sold yourself
to do evil in the eyes of the LORD. 'I am going to bring disaster on

you. I will consume your descendants and cut off from Ahab every
last male in Israel—slave or free. I will make your house like that of
Jeroboam son of Nebat and that of Baasha son of Ahijah, because you
have provoked me to anger and have caused Israel to sin.' "
(21:17–22)

Five or six years had elapsed since the word of the
Lord had come to Elijah. During this time he must have
longed to hear it again. He had no audience and no opportunities for ministry that we're aware of. God was preparing him for just this moment. His simple duty was to stand
and wait, available to serve when God put him to use.

When the time came he was ready. He arose and
went to the vineyard of Naboth just as the king arrived to
gloat over his acquisition. It meant nothing to Elijah that
Ahab's two officers Jehu and Bidkar rode in Ahab's chariot with him (see 2 Kings 9:25). He didn't consider
Jezebel's murderous threats. He went to find Ahab so he
could deliver his message: Have *you* not murdered a man
and seized his property? In the sight of heaven, Ahab was
responsible for the evil he had done and the evil he could
have prevented.

God wants us to loath sin, too—and be its executioner. If we won't, he will!

God judges sin because he loathes what it does to us
and to others. There is no other motive in God, nothing
deeper than his love for us. He wants us to loath sin, too—
and be its executioner. If we won't, he will!

Perhaps with scenes of Mount Carmel still embla-
zoned in his memory, Ahab listened to Elijah. On this occasion, at least, he paid attention.

> *When Ahab heard these words, he tore his clothes, put on sack-*
> *cloth and fasted. He lay in sackcloth and went around meekly.*
> *Then the word of the LORD came to Elijah the Tishbite: "Have*
> *you noticed how Ahab has humbled himself before me? Because he*
> *has humbled himself, I will not bring this disaster in his day."*
> (21:27–29)

Ahab's turning, however, was remorse not repentance. Within a few months the event faded from his mind
and he reverted to type, following Jezebel and her lies. The
light that had flickered at intervals finally died altogether,
and his soul sank into utter darkness. Soon after, he was
killed.

Rejecting the godly counsel of Micaiah the prophet,
Ahab went into battle at Ramoth Gilead against a vastly
superior Syrian army. He went incognito, wearing the garb
of a common soldier, trying to avert the prophet's prediction that he would not return.

The prophet's forecast found him out. "Someone drew
his bow at random and hit the king of Israel between the
sections of his armor" (1 Kings 22:34). This solitary arrow,
lofted into the air in a volley of random shots, "happened"
to pierce Ahab's armor in the tiny gap where the breastplate
was joined to the skirt.

"Lucky shot!" we say. It was one of those odd twists in
life which pass under the category of chance but which,
when closely examined, once again prove to be the hand of
God.

"So the king died and was brought to Samaria, and they buried him there. They washed the chariot at a pool in Samaria (where the prostitutes bathed), and the dogs licked up his blood" (22:37), as Elijah had predicted.

Some time later, Jezebel, too, met her violent, bloody end—despite the fact that God gave her ample time to consider her deeds and repent (2 Kings 9:30–37).

Jezebel was the mother of all malice, violence, and monstrous, disgusting vice. She despised God, trampled underfoot a host of human and divine laws, and breathed her brand of falsehood into Israel's courts, schools, homes, and bedrooms. She corrupted five kings and two kingdoms.

Her son Ahaziah, who succeeded Ahab on the throne, died calling on Beelzebub, the Lord of the flies. Her second son, Jehoram, was no better. Though he removed his mother's phallic symbol from the temple court, he put it in her Baal temple so he could keep all his options open.

Jezebel's daughter was the terrible Athaliah who married Jehoram, the king of Judah, and infected him with Baal worship. (She probably also infected him in other ways. He died of a disorder the symptoms of which are suspiciously like those of a venereal disease.)

After the death of her son, also named Ahaziah, Athaliah reigned over Judah for five years. During her tenure she set out to exterminate the seed of David, an end she almost achieved. She murdered all of David's descendants except the infant Joash, who was hidden from harm by the high priest. Had she succeeded in her slaughter, there would have been no Messiah. David's "lamp" would have been extinguished. This was Jezebel's legacy.

Yet, in mercy, God withheld judgment, waiting for Jezebel to turn. But she never did. In the end she was reduced to ruin, ordered to her death by Jehu, whom she was trying to seduce:

> *Jezebel . . . painted her eyes, arranged her hair and looked out of a window. As Jehu entered the gate, she asked, "Have you come in peace, Zimri, you murderer of your master?"*
>
> *He looked up at the window and called out, "Who is on my side? Who?" Two or three eunuchs looked down at him. "Throw her down!" Jehu said. So they threw her down, and some of her blood spattered the wall and the horses as they trampled her underfoot.*
>
> *Jehu went in and ate and drank. "Take care of that cursed woman," he said, "and bury her, for she was a king's daughter." But when they went out to bury her, they found nothing except her skull, her feet and her hands. They went back and told Jehu, who said, "This is the word of the LORD that he spoke through his servant Elijah the Tishbite: On the plot of ground at Jezreel dogs will devour Jezebel's flesh. Jezebel's body will be like refuse on the ground in the plot at Jezreel, so that no one will be able to say, 'This is Jezebel.' "* (2 Kings 9:30–37)

Though Elijah was not on earth to see it, his prediction of her death was fulfilled right down to the last grim detail.

> *Though the mills of God grind slowly*
> *Yet they grind exceeding small.*
> *Though with patience he stands waiting*
> *With exactness grinds he all.*
>   —Fredrick Von Logau

And then there was the aforementioned Ahaziah, Ahab and Jezebel's terrible spawn:

Ahaziah son of Ahab became king of Israel in Samaria in the seventeenth year of Jehoshaphat king of Judah, and he reigned over Israel for two years. He did evil in the eyes of the LORD, because he walked in the ways of his father and mother and in the ways of Jeroboam son of Nebat, who caused Israel to sin. He served and worshiped Baal and provoked the LORD, the God of Israel, to anger, just as his father had done. (1 Kings 22:51–53)

Ahaziah succeeded to his father and mother's throne—and to their sins. He grew up to be just like his parents. And that was his tragedy.

When God's will is broken, suffering is inevitable.

He was idolatrous and indolent. He shrank from leadership, leading a life of restless self-indulgence until the day he stepped through a lattice in the roof of his palace and fell to the ground. It was no accident; it was a heaven-sent fall. When God's will is broken, suffering is inevitable.

Ahaziah took to his bed and sent messengers to the priests of Baal-Zebub: "Go and consult Baal-Zebub, the god of Ekron," he said, "to see if I will recover from this injury" (2 Kings 1:2).

Baal-Zebub was part of the Phoenician pantheon. He was the patron saint of the sick. One Ugaritic text reads:

> *Who among the gods will drive out malady?*
> *Remove sickness?*
> *None among the Gods answered him.*

When no one answered, Baal-Zebub replied:

> *It is I that will make magic*
> *and I will surely call [health] into being.*
> *It will drive out sickness;*
> *expelling the illness.*

The Jews later interpreted Baal-Zebub's [Beelzebub] name to mean "the Lord of the Flies" and said that he was the prince of demons (Matthew 12:24). Behind Ahaziah's healing god lay the Prince of Darkness.

Ahaziah was thumbing his nose at the God of Israel and choosing the dark side—a choice of ways that had brought God's wrath on his father's house. Such resistance could not go unchallenged.

The Angel of the Lord appeared to Elijah and sent him to intercept Ahaziah's emissaries as they sped across the plains of Esdraelon toward Ekron. His presence arrested them in their tracks: "Is it because there is no God in Israel that you are going off to consult Baal-Zebub, the god of Ekron?" Elijah demanded to know. "Therefore this is what the LORD says: 'You will not leave the bed you are lying on. You will certainly die!' " (2 Kings 1:3–4).

The messengers had no idea who the stranger was. They may have been Phoenicians who had never encountered him before, or it may be that Elijah had been keeping to himself. Either way, they were so awed by his presence and message they determined to return at once to the king. Once again we see the awesome, nation-shaking power of a woman or a man filled and flooded with God.

The messengers found Ahaziah lying on his bed. When they told him the reason for their return, the king asked them, "What kind of man was it who came to meet you and told you this?"

They replied, "He was a man with a garment of hair and with a leather belt round his waist."

"That was Elijah," the king sighed.

Ahaziah, it seems, had heard all the stories. Yet he hadn't learned a thing! He responded to his servants' report by sending an officer with a contingent of fifty soldiers to capture the prophet. He wanted to get Elijah in his hands so he could kill him. This wasn't the first time Elijah's life had been in serious jeopardy.

The officer and his men found the venerable prophet from Tishbe sitting calmly on a hilltop tending to his own business, and the officer said to him, "Man of God, the king says 'Come down!' " (verse 9). He was overstating his mission, speaking with unwarranted insolence. The insult was less against Elijah than it was against Elijah's God.

Elijah answered, "If I am a man of God, may fire come down from heaven and consume you and your fifty men!" (verse 10). The fire of God flamed out from heaven and consumed the captain and his men. There was no personal pique in this judgment, no personal wrong to redress. Elijah was "zealous for the LORD God Almighty"—filled with indignation that God's name had been unhallowed on the earth.

Here again, Elijah was demonstrating Yahweh's ascendancy over Baal. Baal's icons frequently depict him carrying a stylized lightning bolt. It was his primary weapon. In several Ugaritic texts Baal hurls fire from heaven. One reads:

He threw lightning to the earth.

Not to be outdone, Ahaziah sent another officer and another contingent—with the same dreadful result. So, he sent another, but this captain had enough wisdom to respond with reverence and humility. Falling on his knees before Elijah he begged, "Man of God, please have respect for my life and the lives of these fifty men, your servants! See, fire has fallen from heaven and consumed the first two captains and all their men. But now have respect for my life!" (verses 13–14).

> *The angel of the* LORD *said to Elijah, "Go down with him; do not be afraid of him." So Elijah got up and went down with him to the king.*
>
> *He told the king, "This is what the* LORD *says: Is it because there is no God in Israel for you to consult that you have sent messengers to consult Baal-Zebub, the god of Ekron? Because you have done this, you will never leave the bed you are lying on. You will certainly die!"* (verses 15–16)

As Elijah predicted, within a few days Ahaziah died and, dying childless, left his kingdom to his brother Jehoram.

Ahaziah's father, Ahab, reigned for twenty-two long years; Ahaziah reigned for only two. As Bishop Hall observed a long time ago, "Some sinners live long to aggravate their judgment, others die soon to hasten it."

The Great Equalizer

Though it may seem to us at times that the wicked make their way through the world unscathed by their evil, there is a forgotten factor in the equation. That factor is death, the great equalizer. Death stalks men and women relentlessly. "The statistics are very impressive," George

Bernard Shaw grumbled. "One out of every one person dies." There's no escape for anyone once they've been born. "Man is destined to die . . . and after that to face judgment" (Hebrews 9:27). "Payday someday!" Robert G. Lee, a preacher of another era said.

A few years ago I stood in the mummy chamber of the Egyptian Museum and looked down at the shrunken remains of Ramses the Great and said to myself, *Is this the man who terrorized the ancient Near Eastern world?*

Jean Massilon, the French bishop of Clermont, put it well when he looked down on the heads of state of all Europe, gathered in the Cathedral of Notre Dame for the funeral of Louis XIV (who called himself Louis the Great). "Brethren," said the bishop, "in the hour of death, no one is great." Nothing settles the score quite like death.

One of Israel's poets struggled with the issue of the evil that people do that is not requited in their lifetimes. They "have no struggles," he grumbled:

> *Their bodies are healthy and strong.*
> *They are free from the burdens common to man;*
>> *they are not plagued by human ills.*
> *Therefore pride is their necklace;*
>> *they clothe themselves with violence.*
> *From their callous hearts comes iniquity;*
>> *the evil conceits of their minds know no limits.*
> *They scoff, and speak with malice;*
>> *in their arrogance they threaten oppression.*
> *Their mouths lay claim to heaven,*
>> *and their tongues take possession of the earth.*
> *Therefore their people turn to them*
>> *and drink up waters in abundance.*

They say, "How can God know?
Does the Most High have knowledge?"
This is what the wicked are like—
always carefree, they increase in wealth.

—Psalm 73:4–12

The godless scoff at God, persecute his people, and get away with murder, the poet complained. "Surely in vain have I kept my heart pure" (verse 13).

But then the psalmist recalled the fact of death and destruction:

Surely, you place them on slippery ground;
you cast them down to ruin.
How suddenly are they destroyed,
completely swept away by terrors!
As a dream when one awakes,
so when you arise, O LORD,
you will despise them as fantasies.

—verses 18–20

The ungodly are on a slippery slope to the grave; they are cast down to ruin, they are destroyed, they are completely swept away by terrors!

The Hebrew word for "terrors" is a poetic designation for the abode of the dead—a place of speechless desolation and destruction. There, as Lewis said, they "will be left utterly and absolutely outside, repelled, exiled, estranged, finally and unspeakably ignored!"

"Don't be deceived," Paul wrote, "God cannot be mocked. A man reaps what he sows. The one who sows to please his sinful nature, from that nature will reap destruction" (Galatians 6:7).

Paul wrote again to those who have thumbed their noses at God:

> *Do you think you will escape God's judgment? Or do you show contempt for the riches of his kindness, tolerance and patience, not realizing that God's kindness leads you toward repentance?*
>
> *But because of your stubbornness and your unrepentant heart, you are storing up wrath against yourself for the day of God's wrath, when his righteous judgment will be revealed. God "will give to each person according to what he has done."* (Romans 2:3–6)

God yearns over sinful men and women with unutterable sorrow.

God yearns over sinful men and women with unutterable sorrow. "There is not a dying sparrow in the recesses of the deepest woods over whose last agonies the Almighty does not bend with sympathetic interest and alleviating tenderness; so there is not one waif of humanity excluded from the warm zone of His infinite compassion and tender pity" (Meyer). God's love lingers over every lost soul.

There is no one God will save against his or her will.

"How can I give you up, Ephraim?" God said of Israel through his tears. "How can I hand you over, Israel? How can I treat you like Admah? How can I make you like Zeboiim? My heart is changed within me; all my compassion is aroused" (Hosea 11:8).

There is no one that God will not save, *but there is no one he will save against his or her will.* His patience endures as long as there is the slightest hope of repentance, but if people do not want God's love, then he will not foist it on them. In that sense, hell, though it seems odd to say it, may be just another provision of God's love. He loves us enough to leave us alone.

But understand what that means—eternal life without law, without love, without laughter, without beauty, without any of the elements that make life worthwhile. God is the giver of every good and perfect gift and the source of everything that is good and true and beautiful. His absence means the absence of everything that gives meaning to existence. If that's what hell is, then Lewis was right: hell is exactly the right name for what it would be.

Sons of Thunder

Each time I read this segment of Elijah's story I'm reminded of the day our Lord was passing through Samaria on his way to Jerusalem. He sent messengers ahead to prepare a place, but the people of Samaria rejected him.

When James and John heard about the refusal they fumed, "Lord, do you want us to call fire down from heaven to destroy them?" (Luke 9:54). They had been on the Mount of Transfiguration and had seen their Lord with Moses and Elijah. Elijah and his fiery judgment was fresh in their minds. But when they asked for similar judgment, Jesus turned and rebuked them.

Later manuscripts add an explanatory statement, supplying the content of the rebuke: "You do not know what kind of spirit you are of, for the Son of Man did not come to destroy men's lives, but to save them."

Whether the addition is a scribal emendation or belongs to the text, I leave to scholars to decide. I do think, however, that it accurately reflects Jesus' thoughts. It is not our business to judge God's enemies. He treads out the winepress of his wrath *alone* (see Isaiah 63:3). Our business is to bring salvation to the world.

Paul writes,

> *Leave room for God's wrath, for it is written: 'It is* mine *to avenge; I will repay,' says the Lord. On the contrary: 'If your enemy is hungry, feed him; if he is thirsty, give him something to drink. In doing this, you will heap burning coals on his head.' Do not be overcome by evil, but overcome evil with good"* (Romans 12:19–21, emphasis added).

I think of the day that Jesus' disciples reported to him the Pharisees' bitter opposition. He replied, "Every plant that my heavenly Father has not planted will be pulled up by the roots. Leave them [alone]" (Matthew 15:13–14).

Our task is to overwhelm them with love— and save them if we can.

That's godly advice. It's not our task to root out evil men and women; our task is to overwhelm them with love—feed them, give them something to drink, and save them if we can.

"Be merciful to those who doubt," Jude wrote, "snatch others from the fire and save them; to others show mercy, mixed with fear—hating even the clothing stained by corrupted flesh" (Jude 22–23).

Some unbelievers are close to salvation but still unconvinced. Persuade them.

Others are close to destruction. Snatch them from the fire and save them if you can.

Still others—the saddest of all—have hardened their hearts against the truth and will not be influenced. Have mercy on them mixed with fear: there but for the grace of God go you and I.

Despise the garments contaminated by sin, but don't despise the sinners! Show them compassion, and love them to the end. They are not our enemies; they're tragic victims of a terrible, merciless enemy, taken captive by him to do his will (see 2 Timothy 2:26).

But "if love will not compel them to come in, we must leave them to God, the judge of all," John Wesley said. "Will not the Judge of all the earth do right?" (Genesis 18:25).

It's that assurance that keeps us steady in the face of all the evil that men and women do. It's that unshakable truth to which we may cling as the Enemy's shadow falls over our nation and culture. We can take evil seriously, but we needn't panic in the face of its steady advance. Why? Because we know that God's processes are perfectly adequate to deal with the worst that perverse and villainous people can do. That confidence results in poise in the face of appalling, disorienting disorder. The oft-quoted motto to the contrary, you can keep your head when all others are losing theirs, because you *do* understand the situation.

Saint John of the Cross said that those who know God and what he is doing have three distinguishing characteristics—tranquillity, gentleness, and strength. That suggests to me an immense depth, an invulnerable steadiness, an ability to respond with kindness and care for others out of a center of quiet rest.

Frenzy, fury, hysteria, intensity, impatience, instability, pessimism, and every other kind of fuss and ferocity are marks of an immature soul. Those who know that "God works in tranquillity," as one old saint put it, are not like that. They share the calm and quiet nature of the One "who works out *everything* in conformity with the purpose of his will" (Ephesians 1:11, emphasis added).

> God is working out his purpose
> 　　'spite of all that happens here
> Lawless nations in commotion,
> 　　restless like a storm-tossed ocean
> He controls their rage and fury
> 　　so his children need not fear,
> Let our hearts then turn to heaven
> 　　where he bides his time in peace
> Giving him our heart's devotion
> 　　till the present troubles cease.
>
> 　　　　　　　—Author Unknown

Seeing Deeper

1. Naboth's vineyard—just a small piece of real estate, just a tiny corner of Israel with some potential for a vegetable garden. Yet Ahab's desire for that land grew beyond all reasonable proportions. What were Ahab's reactions to Naboth's unwillingness to sell? And what was the end result?

   Can you cite other tragedies—perhaps in your own experience—that resulted from a man or a woman

becoming blinded by desire? How can our own thinking become distorted by unchecked desires?

2. In 1 Kings 21:27–29, Ahab shows a surprising—if temporary—change of attitude. The author calls Ahab's
   response remorse rather than repentance. What's the
   difference? Can you discern the difference in yourself?
   What does God's response to this episode tell you about
   our heavenly Father's heart?

3. Read 1 Kings 22:1–28. Ahab confronts another man of
   God. Did he know who Micaiah was? Did he seek
   wisdom or guidance from him? Why did he have such
   contempt for the prophet?

   Now turn to 2 Kings 1:1–14. How did Ahaziah,
   Ahab's son, interact with the man of God? What
   might have been behind the king's steadfast refusal
   to turn to God?

4. For whatever superficial success they might have
   enjoyed in their wicked careers, Ahab, Jezebel, and
   Ahaziah didn't reckon on one forgotten factor. What
   was that ultimate factor? Turn to Luke 16:19–31;
   Hebrews 9:27; and 1 Peter 4:3–5. Death brings no second chances. Would we reflect Jesus more brightly if we
   more frequently pondered the fate awaiting our lost
   neighbors and friends?

5. "Some unbelievers are close to salvation but still not
   convinced. Persuade them. Others are close to destruction. Snatch them from the fire."

a. What names come to your mind as you ponder each of these categories?

b. Whom might you enlist to pray with you and hold you accountable to speak to these lost individuals?

Elisha saw the invisible hosts of God. He had learned that most important lesson of all—he had learned to put his eyes on that world that cannot be seen. So it is with us: There is a reality all about us that does not register on our retinas. We will always be disadvantaged, but we can never be overcome. Our awareness of the unseen world will maintain our hearts in strength and courage in the day of pressure and panic. It is the means by which weaklings are turned into mighty warriors and rout whole armies. It's the way by which you and I take hold of strength.

Chapter Eleven

Seeing What Cannot Be Seen

Are there no things—I mean things—but what we see?
—C. S. Lewis

Elijah was getting "old and timey," as my grandkids used to say.

Life had taken away his youth, but God had given in exchange great calm and truth. The prophet's zeal for holiness had been tempered through the years by suffering and deep reflection. Wisdom had softened his face. Now, at the end of his career, he was given a time of comparative calm in which to entrust to others what God had entrusted to him.

"Time hath a taming hand," John Newton said. Age breaks down our energy and strength and prevents us from too much activity. We have more time for contemplation and prayer. As we draw nearer to things to come, things present lose their grip on us. We're more inclined to lean on God. His nearness rubs off on us; we reflect more of his invisible presence.

In time our influence takes on a peculiar power. Tested character and God-ripened experience have a seasoned vitality and vision that busier youth cannot have. "The older a man is," said Henry Durbanville, "the better he is—the broader his vision, the saner and wiser his outlook, the more mature his opinions."

Not *all* old-timers are wise, of course. There are wise old folks and there are wicked old folks and some folks just get to be old fools. But since all knowledge, wisdom, and character are cumulative, it follows that those who have loved the Savior and walked with him through time will reach maturity rich in their understanding of God and wise in his ways.

"Old men ought to be explorers," T. S. Eliot said. Getting older doesn't mean becoming obsolete. It can mean growing, maturing, serving, ministering, venturing, enjoying ourselves to the end of our days. "Have a blast while you last," a friend of mine says.

To idle away our last years is to rob ourselves of the best years of our lives—and to rob the church of one of the choicest gifts that God has given to enrich it. He still sends his servants into the marketplace in the eleventh hour. There is still service to be rendered, battles to be fought, and victories to be won. Even when old and gray, we can declare God's "power to the next generation, [his] might to all who are to come" (Psalm 71:18).

Older folks may not have the energy or inclination for leadership, but they are an invaluable asset to the next generation of leaders. They should be on tap not on top. There comes a time when our greatest usefulness is passing on our understanding to others.

Wesley was asked once what he would do if he knew he had only a short time to live: "I should meet with my preachers," he said, "till the moment came that I was called to yield my spirit back to Him that gave it."

Elijah, a kindred soul, met with his preachers in the schools established at Bethel, Gilgal, and Jericho—places of light and learning—and spent his last days nurturing them. These young men were the so-called sons of the prophets. Elijah, like the abbot of a medieval monastery, was their "father" (2 Kings 2:12).

Of all Elijah's "sons," Elisha was closest to his father. Handpicked by the older man, his relationship with Elijah went all the way back to Sinai.

God's work has to be done, but it doesn't have to be done by us.

At Sinai, God had given Elijah three assignments: to anoint Hazael king of Syria, Jehu king of Israel, and Elisha as his prophetic successor. Hazael, Jehu, and Elisha combined their efforts to bring Ahab and Jezebel to their knees; they finished the work Elijah began—all of which suggests a hopeful conclusion: God's work has to be done, *but it doesn't have to be done by us.*

Of the three final jobs God gave Elijah, the man from Tishbe only got around to the last one: the calling of Elisha. The other tasks were accomplished by Elisha after Elijah's departure. (The oft-expressed idea that Elijah anointed Hazael and Jehu secretly and Elisha only confirmed their election is precluded by the account of Jehu's anointing in 2 Kings 9.)

The story of Elisha's call is told in 1 Kings 19:19–21:

Elijah went . . . and found Elisha son of Shaphat. [Elisha] was plowing with twelve yoke of oxen, and he himself was driving the twelfth pair. Elijah went up to him and threw his cloak around him. Elisha then left his oxen and ran after Elijah. "Let me kiss my father and mother good-by," he said, "and then I will come with you."

"Go back," Elijah replied. "What have I done to you?"

So Elisha left him and went back. He took his yoke of oxen and slaughtered them. He burned the plowing equipment to cook the meat and gave it to the people, and they ate. Then he set out to follow Elijah and became his attendant.

As Elijah made his way through Galilee, he came to the small town of Abel Maholah. *Abel Maholah* means "meadow of dancing" and suggests the joy that accompanied the rich harvests that characterized that region. There was a prosperous farmer there, a man named Shaphat, who had vast holdings in the area. A wealthy man, his fields stretched as far as the eye could see.

The drought that had plagued Israel for three and a half years was broken, and Shaphat's workers were preparing the fields for seed. Elisha, Shaphat's son, occupied a privileged position on the farm. But like all dutiful sons in Israel, he did his share of the dirty work. When we first see him, he is "driving the twelfth" of twelve pairs of oxen, eating the dust of eleven plows turning the soil in front of him.

The old prophet slipped up behind Elisha while he was plowing, cast his rough, camel-hair mantle over the young farmer's shoulders, and then moved on. Not a word was spoken, but Elisha *knew*. Back then a teacher's mantle stood for all the teacher stood for and suggested an investiture of his authority. "When a great teacher died," Sir John Malcolm wrote in his history of this region, "he bequeathed his patched mantle to the disciple he most esteemed. . . . His mantle was his all and its transfer marked out his heir."

Elisha's response was immediate: He left his oxen standing where they were and ran after Elijah with only one request: "Let me kiss my father and mother good-by," he said, "and then I will come with you." (Matthew Henry observed that Elisha returned "to *take* leave, not to *ask* leave of them.")

Elijah's response sounds stern and unrelenting: "Go back [return]. What have I done to you?" But he meant no severity. Elijah was giving Elisha permission to return to his father and mother if he wanted to do so. The words, "What have I done to you?" invited thoughtful inquiry. Elijah wanted Elisha to think about the implications of what he was about to do—to count the cost of his call. He understood the sacrifice that the younger man was being asked to make, and he wanted to leave Elisha uncoerced, his service the outcome of his own heart's conviction and choice.

Elisha chose to forsake mother and father and houses and lands—and follow. It is highly significant that his oxen, the yoke, and the wooden plowshare—all implements related to his past life—were consumed in a final feast with his family and friends. In an odd mix of metaphors, he burned his bridges and ate them!

Then "[Elisha] set out to follow Elijah and became his attendant." For many years after, the young man did little more than "pour water on the hands of Elijah" as the idiom has it (2 Kings 3:11). Yet he listened and learned, determined to let none of Elijah's words fall to the ground.

Elisha stuck to Elijah like a limpet, fully willing to share his mentor's dangers and privations. In turn, Elijah invested himself in Elisha, strengthening the younger man's grip on God and extending his grasp of invisible realities, teaching him, encouraging him. The old prophet knew there was no better way to spend his final days.

It is worth noting that God was preparing Elisha even while Elijah was begging to die. "Take my life, Lord," Elijah had lamented under the desert broom tree. "I'm no use to anyone anymore. I'm a failure—and too old to start over. There's nothing left for me to do but die." The old prophet thought his work was done when, in fact, he was about to enter into his most enduring work—helping to shape a young man whom God intended to use for the next fifty years.

But all earthly good things must come to an end. God informed Elijah that he was sending his chariot to bring him home. Elijah, knowing his departure was imminent, tried to dissuade Elisha from following:

> "Stay here; the LORD has sent me to Bethel."
>
> But Elisha said, "As surely as the LORD lives and as you live, I will not leave you." So they went down to Bethel.
>
> The company of the prophets at Bethel came out to Elisha and asked, "Do you know that the LORD is going to take your master from you today?"
>
> "Yes, I know," Elisha replied, "but do not speak of it." [Don't tell me!]

*Then Elijah said to him, "Stay her, Elisha; the LORD has sent me
to Jericho."*

*And he replied, "As surely as the LORD lives and as you live, I
will not leave you." So they went to Jericho.*

*The company of the prophets at Jericho went up to Elisha and
asked him, "Do you know that the LORD is going to take your master from you today?"*

"Yes, I know," he replied, "but do not speak of it."

*Then Elijah said to him, "Stay here; the LORD has sent me to the
Jordan."*

*And he replied, "As surely as the LORD lives and as you live, I
will not leave you." So the two of them walked on.*   (2 Kings 2:2–6)

Three times Elijah tried to tear himself away from
Elisha. Three times Elisha refused to turn back, affirming
again and again his love for his mentor and his intention to
learn from him as long as he lived—right up to the last bit-
tersweet moment. Old saints, he knew, never outlive their
usefulness.

Elisha followed Elijah from their residence in Gilgal to
Bethel and down the steep descent to Jericho and on to the
banks of the Jordan. When they reached the river, Elijah,
knowing God's will lay on the other side, took off his mantle, "rolled it up and struck the water with it. The water
divided to the right and to the left, and the two of them
crossed over on dry ground" (2:8).

Three times the historian tells us of their camaraderie:
"the two of them walked on"; "the two of them stood by the
Jordan"; "the two of them crossed over on dry ground."
Elijah and Elisha walked together for the last time across
the plain of the Jordan and up the other side. Eventually the
haze or the hills beyond hid the receding figures from the

gaze of the prophets who had accompanied them from Jericho.

Israel's historian drew a veil over most of that last conversation, contenting himself with Elijah's question:

Elijah said to Elisha, "Tell me, what can I do for you before I am taken from you?" (verse 9)

Here's a door flung wide open—a chancy carte blanche—but the older prophet knew his disciple would not ask for a gift that God could not or would not bestow.

Elijah's confidence was well placed: Elisha did not ask for fame, wealth, or earthly power but rather for spiritual influence:

"Let me inherit a double portion of your spirit," Elisha replied.

Elisha asked for the right stuff: a "double portion" of Elijah's spirit—the inheritance of a firstborn son (Deuteronomy 21:17). *Spirit* can mean many things, but here Elisha is using the term in the sense of a dominant disposition. Elisha wanted to be the heir of the disposition or attitude that enabled Elijah to touch lives so deeply.

"You have asked a difficult thing," Elijah said, "yet if you see me when I am taken from you, it will be yours—otherwise not."

As they were walking along and talking together, suddenly a chariot of fire and horses of fire appeared and separated the two of them, and Elijah went up to heaven in a whirlwind. Elisha saw this and cried out, "My father! My father! The chariots and horsemen of Israel!" And Elisha saw him no more. Then he took hold of his own clothes and tore them apart. (2 Kings 2:10–12)

Elijah's requirement that Elisha see his departure seems frivolous, but it was not. It had to do with that all-important ability to see what otherwise cannot be seen.

"Elijah was a man just like us," James said. His power came not from some latent or inherent human ability but because his eyes were fixed on what Paul describes as "what is unseen" (2 Corinthians 4:18). That was the secret of his influence. The real issue in Elijah's "test" was whether or not Elisha had learned his secret.

Indeed, the younger prophet had learned the lesson well. Meyer wrote, "No mere mortal eye could have beheld the fiery cortege. To senses dulled by materialism, the space occupied by the flaming seraphim would have seemed devoid of any special interest, and bare as the rest of the surrounding scenery."

A mere human would have seen nothing but the sudden disappearance of the prophet—yet Elisha saw the invisible hosts of God. He had learned that most important lesson of all, that truth that informs every other truth, without which nothing else matters: *He had learned to put his eyes on that world that cannot be seen.*

And so it is with us: There is a reality all about us that does not register on our retinas. "The angel of the LORD encamps around those who fear him, and he delivers them" (Psalm 34:7). We cannot normally see those encampments, but—whether we see them or not—they are certainly there. "Hell is nigh, but God is nigher; Circling us with hosts of fire."

> *It lies around us like a cloud—*
> *A world we do not see.*
>   —Harriet Beecher Stowe

In a materialistic world like ours, the only real things are the things we can detect with our five senses. "What you see is what you get," in the words of that old philosopher Flip Wilson.

There is another realm—more substantial than anything we can see, hear, touch, taste, smell.

There is, however, another realm or reality—more actual, more factual, more substantial than anything we can see, hear, touch, taste, smell in this world. It exists all around us—not out there somewhere, but *here*.

There are legions of angels at our disposal, for which earth's forces have no countermeasures. "The chariots of God are tens of thousands and thousands of thousands" (Psalm 68:17). God and his squadrons of angels are everywhere around us—an encircling fire. We cannot see them with our natural eyes, but whether we see them or not, they are there. The earth is crammed with them!

There are legions of angels at our disposal, for which earth's forces have no countermeasures.

Faith is the means by which we gain access to that invisible world. That is belief's true function. Faith is to the spiritual realm what the five senses are to the natural. It is the means by which we grasp spiritual reality and bring it into the realm of our experience. "Faith," said the writer of

Hebrews, "is being sure of what we hope for and certain of what we do not see" (11:1).

Faith is simpler and grander than we believe. We tend to think of it as psyching ourselves into accepting improbable facts that are hard, if not impossible, to believe. But authentic faith is something else: It is the capacity to look beyond the seen to the unseen world of reality where the invisible God is at work. The heroes of the book of Hebrews were not folks who believed what others could not believe. They were women and men who saw what others could not see! They "quenched the fury of the flames, and escaped the edge of the sword; whose weakness was turned to strength; and who became powerful in battle and routed foreign armies." Why? How? Because they "saw him who is invisible" (verse 27).

They saw God at work behind the scenes and that was what enabled them to do what God was asking them to do.

Seeing always precedes doing. Consider Jesus' disciple Nathanael, sitting under his fig tree. Our Lord said of him, "Here is a true Israelite, in whom there is nothing false" (John 1:47). Nathanael was amazed, and he believed.

Then hear what Jesus said: " 'You believe because I told you I saw you under the fig tree. You shall *see* greater things than that.' He then added, 'I tell you the truth, you shall *see* heaven open, and the angels of God ascending and descending on the Son of Man' " (verses 50–51, emphasis added).

The main thing is to grow eyes that *see*. Berra noted, "You can observe a lot by seeing."

Where Is the God of Elijah?

As soon as Elijah departed, Elisha "picked up the cloak that had fallen from Elijah and went back and stood on the bank of the Jordan. Then he took the cloak [the symbol of Elijah's prophetic office to which he succeeded] . . . and struck the water with it. [It's not clear from our English translations, but the Hebrew text suggests the act accomplished nothing; the waters were not parted! Elijah's mantle had failed.]

"Where now is the LORD, the God of Elijah?" Elisha cried (2 Kings 2: 13–14).

Good question. How often have we raised that cry when we have stood face-to-face with some obstruction? (Often there's more despair than query in the question.)

But with the question came the answer: "I am *here!*" Elijah had gone home, but God remained—more alive than Elisha could ever imagine.

It is what he does. If you ask where God is, he will answer you, "I am here with you"—always at hand—to do for you what he has done for others in the past.

All power comes from that invisible realm that only faith can see.

There is no power in the prophet's mantle, his manner, or his methods. There is nothing peculiar to an individual that qualifies anyone for the task God has given her or him to do. All power comes from that invisible realm that only faith can see.

And so Elisha fixed his eyes once more on what is unseen. With sight restored (it must be restored again and again), he struck the water and, "It divided to the right and to the left, and he crossed over.

"The company of the prophets from Jericho, who were watching, said 'The spirit of Elijah is resting on Elisha.' And they went to meet him and bowed to the ground before him" (2 Kings 2:14–15).

There Are More of Us Than There Are of Them!

An incident took place later in Elisha's career that affirms he had learned how to see.

It happened like this: Josephus, the Jewish historian, wrote that the Syrian king Ben-Hadad was trying his best to capture and kill King Jehoram of Israel, who often hunted along the border between the two nations. At that time, the Jordan Valley was heavily wooded and a prime habitat for lions and bears and other wild animals.

Elisha, however, was privy to everything Ben-Hadad planned and kept Jehoram informed so that the king was able to avoid being ambushed.

Ben-Hadad suspected skullduggery and summoned his officers to locate the informant. "Will you not tell me which of us is on the side of the king of Israel?" he asked (2 Kings 6:11).

" 'None of us, my lord the king,' said one of his officers, 'but Elisha, the prophet who is in Israel, tells the king of Israel the very words you speak in your bedroom' " (verse 12).

Ben-Hadad's bedroom was bugged!

God overheard the king's pillow talk, gathered fresh intelligence each night, and passed it on to Elisha.

" 'Go, find out where he is,' the king ordered, 'so I can send men and capture him' " (verse 13).

Elisha wasn't hard to find because he wasn't trying to hide. The Syrian scouts quickly discovered he was temporar-

ily residing in the city of Dothan. When they reported back to
Ben-Hadad he "sent horses and chariots and a strong force"
(verse 14). Big numbers is a typically pagan notion of power.

Dothan was a tiny settlement about twelve miles north
of Samaria. Excavations there have uncovered a village
about ten to twelve acres in size. The only wall then was a
stone rampart from an earlier period that was still in use
and, as ancient walls go, was unimpressive. There had never
been anything strategic in Dothan worth defending—until
Elisha showed up.

The Syrian army gathered by night, surrounded the
city, sized up the defenders and the walls, and decided
there was nothing much to be concerned about. They bed-
ded down and waited for the dawn.

Early the next morning, Elisha's servant awakened
and began making preparations to return to their residence
in Samaria. He happened to look over the wall, and he discovered to his great dismay that "an army with horses and
chariots had surrounded the city. 'Oh, my lord, what shall
we do?' the servant asked" (verse 15). Elisha comforted his
servant with a word:

> "Don't be afraid," the prophet answered. "Those who are with us
> are more than those who are with them."
>
> And Elisha prayed, "O LORD, open his eyes so he may see." Then
> the LORD opened the servant's eyes, and he looked and saw the hills
> full of horses and chariots of fire all around Elisha. (verses 16–17)

He saw the legions of heaven at Elisha's disposal.

"We've got 'em outnumbered!" Elisha assured his
frazzled and frightened servant. "There are more of us than
there are of them!"

And so it is: Forces gather around us in opposition; our opponents always seem to have the edge. But all that is false. We are never outnumbered. We are never outmanned or outgunned.

Our opponents always seem to have the edge. But all that is false.

"*Many* are my foes," David wrote. "*Many* rise up against me. . . . [Nevertheless] I lie down and sleep; I wake again, because the LORD sustains me. I will not fear the tens of thousands drawn up against me on every side" (Psalm 3:1, 5–6, emphasis added).

We will always be disadvantaged, but we can never be overcome. Our awareness of the unseen world will maintain our hearts in strength and courage in the day of pressure and panic. It is the means by which weaklings are turned into mighty warriors and by which they rout whole armies. It's the way by which you and I can take hold of strength.

Most of us remember what it feels like to be outnumbered:

> when you walk into a crowded room and feel intimidated and insecure
>
> when you're in a classroom full of hostile thinking and you're the only one who takes God seriously
>
> when you find yourself the sole voice for morality and righteousness
>
> when you feel squashed and crushed by overwhelming odds

Whenever you find yourself in that sort of situation, you must say to yourself, "The Lord and his legions are here! There are more of us than there are of them!"

Of course there will be privations, difficulties, trials, but the answer to all is that vision.

There is no situation too difficult.

There is no fear that cannot be dispelled.

There is no opponent that cannot be quelled.

God is there with you in that place; you are on holy ground. Though nations conspire and people plot against you, God is between you and all opposition. However strong the foe, God is stronger. However swift the blow, God is swifter and can ward it off. When the enemy comes in like a flood, the Spirit of God will raise up a standard against him.

> *"No weapon forged against you will prevail,*
> *and you will refute every tongue that accuses you,*
> *This is the heritage of the servants of the* LORD,
> *and this is their vindication from me," declares the* LORD.
> —Isaiah 54:17

Seeing God "invests a Christian worker with the awful atmosphere of God," said Charles Fox. "But such transformation belongs to none but the seer, for the seer of the unseen is the only true seer. The best seers, not the best sayers, are God's most effective messengers."

And so you must grow eyes that see. They are a gift of God given in answer to prayer. So Paul prayed that the eyes of our hearts may be enlightened that we may see what otherwise cannot be seen (Ephesians 1:18).

Your seeing will grow as you feed on God's Word: "Faith comes from hearing the message," Paul assured us

(Romans 10:17). The test of your time in the Word is this: Has it enabled you to see?

"Seeing depends on where you stand," Lewis observed. "It also depends on the sort of person you are." Purity of heart enables perceptions that others cannot duplicate. It gets glimpses of the workings of God where duplicity detects nothing. "Blessed are the pure in heart," Jesus said, "for they [and they alone] will see God" (Matthew 5:8).

Together, then, let us ask our Lord to give us eyes that "pierce to the further brink of things we cannot see" (MacDonald).

Then you will have no reason to ask, "Where is the Lord God of Elijah?" You will know that he is with you, waiting to do as much for you as he did for Elijah. So you will become the heir of those "who through faith conquered kingdoms, administered justice, and gained what was promised" (Hebrews 11:33).

Seeing Deeper

1. Read again the account of Elisha's calling in 1 Kings 19:19–21. What do you see in this passage that reveals Elisha's character?

2. What legacy did Elisha request of his father in the faith? For what purpose? Why was it important that Elisha actually see his mentor's departure?

3. In 2 Kings 6:13–17, Elisha and his servant viewed the same scene with different eyes. As you reflect on this

account, what could you learn about viewing your own encounters with immovable obstacles and overwhelming circumstances?

Read 2 Corinthians 4:16–18 and try to restate Paul's perspective in your own words.

4. The author states: "The heroes of the book of Hebrews were not folks who believed what others could not believe, they were men and women who saw what others could not see." And he adds, "The best seers, not the best sayers, are God's most effective messengers." What might he mean by that? Do you agree? Why?

5. The author tells us that with age, experience, and time with the Lord, "His nearness rubs off on us; we reflect more of his invisible presence." Can you think of one person who stands out in your mind because of the way he or she reflects Jesus Christ? Describe that individual. How could you become more like that man or that woman?

6. After reading the amazing account of Elijah's ministry, we're told in James that Elijah was an individual just like us. A regular person. An ordinary human being. What, then, accounts for his strategic, nation-shaping ministry and the unique place he holds in history?

Note to the Reader

The publisher invites you to share your response to the message of this book by writing Discovery House Publishers, Box 3566, Grand Rapids, MI 49501, USA. For information about other Discovery House books, music, or videos, contact us at the same address or call 1-800-653-8333. Find us on the Internet at http://www.dhp.org/ or send e-mail to books@dhp.org.